Palgrave Studies in Cultural Participation

Series Editors
Andrew Miles
Department of Sociology
University of Manchester
Manchester, UK

Lisanne Gibson
Loughborough University
Loughborough, UK

This series will provide a platform for contributions to a newly defined field of 'participation studies' (Miles and Gibson, forthcoming 2021). Participation in cultural activities is a research subject within a number of disciplines and fields, ranging from sociology to cultural studies, incorporating tourism, leisure heritage, museum, media, theatre, and cultural policy, to business and management studies. This series will bring together debates across these disciplines to consider the subject of cultural participation in all its dimensions.

The series brings together research on traditional cultural tastes and practices with research on informal 'everyday' activities. In doing so it broadens our understanding of cultural participation, focusing on participation as a pluralistic concern, exploring the links between the cultural, civic and social dimensions of participation, and reconsidering its framing in time and space by political economy, material resource and cultural governance.

Riie Heikkilä

Understanding Cultural Non-Participation in an Egalitarian Context

palgrave
macmillan

Riie Heikkilä
Faculty of Social Sciences
Tampere University
Tampere, Finland

ISSN 2661-8699   ISSN 2661-8702   (electronic)
Palgrave Studies in Cultural Participation
ISBN 978-3-031-18864-0   ISBN 978-3-031-18865-7   (eBook)
https://doi.org/10.1007/978-3-031-18865-7

Cover pattern © Melisa Hasan

This Palgrave Macmillan imprint is published by the registered company Springer Nature
Switzerland AG.
The registered company address is: Gewerbestrasse 11, 6330 Cham, Switzerland

The original version of this book was previously published without open access. A correction to this book is available at https://doi.org/10.1007/978-3-031-18865-7_9.

Acknowledgements

Many people have provided invaluable support for this book. Starting chronologically from the launch of my *Understanding Cultural Disengagement in Contemporary Finland* research project in autumn 2017, I want to thank Alan Warde and Tally Katz-Gerro, who acted as hosts during my first academic stay at the University of Manchester in 2018. They provided me valuable opportunities to present my very early work and offered me food for thought and good advice in the moment that I needed it the most. I also wish to thank Luis Enrique Alonso, who hosted me during my second academic stay at the Universidad Autónoma de Madrid in 2019 and always gave me brilliant ideas and readings.

Early drafts of work published in this book have been presented at several conferences, most importantly at the ESA Sociology of Consumption Sociology of Consumption Research network, at the ISA Research Committee of Sociology of Leisure and at the Finnish Westermarck Society's Consumption and Culture network. Thank you for all your friendly and constructive comments and cooperation along the years, especially Anna-Mari Almila, Predrag Cvetičanin, David Inglis, Susanne Janssen, Nina Kahma, Irmak Karademir Hazir, Shintaro Kono, Frédéric Lebaron, Adrian Leguina, Maaria Linko, Nete Nørgaard Kristensen, Andrew Miles, Eva Myrczik and Marc Verboord, but also many others.

A permanent sheet anchor is Semi Purhonen, who has tirelessly supported me and my various projects in countless occasions, both on and off work. Thank you for that! In this same occasion, I wish to thank our PhD students, especially Jarmo Kallunki, Ossi Sirkka and Sara Sivonen, who have provided clever ideas and many great occasions to brainstorm together. I also want to thank all the members of the KuSoSe seminar Semi has been leading—thank you everybody for reading the early drafts of these chapters. Likewise, I am very grateful to Anu Katainen and Taru Lindblom, who have offered their expertise, as excellent co-writers, to some of the publications that served as fundamental stepping-stones when preparing this book. I also especially want to thank Keijo Rahkonen and Jukka Gronow, who took time to read the final manuscript with great detail and wonderful comments that made my arguments much sharper. Both were my PhD directors back in time, so revising this book with them was for me like a precious opportunity to travel back to early academic years.

Finally, I am deeply grateful to all my interviewees who whole-heartedly opened parts of their lives and minds to me in contexts that were not always easy to navigate for neither party. Properly understanding and making sociology out of the often invisible logics of cultural non-participation would not have been possible without their initial willingness to talk to me. Likewise, I extend warm thanks to the many friends that miraculously helped me find suitable interviewees, a task that would have been impossible to carry out alone.

The research project on cultural non-participation in Finland that this book is based on was supported financially by the Academy of Finland (grant number 307756) and the Finnish Cultural Foundation. The actual writing of the book was made possible through the support of Kone Foundation. I warmly wish to thank all three funders for giving me the opportunity to work on the topics that fascinate me the most.

Additional thanks go to my closest friends who stoically tolerated my talk about the challenges of cultural non-participation for all these years (without much resistance!), my always supportive parents Timo and Säde, my three little brothers, my endlessly encouraging and patient husband Carlos—a past and future co-writer of many sociological texts—and my daughters Iris and Astrid, who provided non-stop cheerful girl power in the house.

CONTENTS

ABOUT THE AUTHOR

Riie Heikkilä is a Docent of Sociology at the Faculty of Social Sciences at Tampere University, Finland. Her main research interests include cultural and social stratification, the links between cultural consumption and production, and the mechanisms behind unequal distribution of cultural capital. She has published widely on these topics in journals such as *The Sociological Review*, *New Media & Society* and *American Journal of Cultural Sociology*. Her most recent book is *Enter Culture, Exit Arts? The Transformation of Cultural Hierarchies in European Newspaper Culture Sections, 1960–2010* (2019, together with Semi Purhonen, Irmak Karademir Hazir, Tina Lauronen, Carlos Jesús Fernández Rodríguez and Jukka Gronow).

PART I

Situating the Research

CHAPTER 1

Introduction

Abstract This chapter is an introduction to the book, a qualitative research about cultural non-participation in an egalitarian society. It introduces the main dilemma: that active cultural participation is linked to high education and class position across different national contexts and that cultural non-participation is typically presented as a problem. The theoretical framework on cultural practices corresponding to social class and being able to generate cultural capital, building on the work of Pierre Bourdieu and his main critics, is explained in detail. Finland, as a fruitful empirical context for the study, is presented. This chapter presents the main research questions on (1) how the cultural participation of hypothetically 'non-participating' groups is and (2) what kinds of symbolic boundaries they draw while talking about their cultural participation.

Keywords Cultural participation • Cultural non-participation • Symbolic boundaries • Finland

A cultural divide is said to be separating our Western societies into two diverging life-worlds that are differentiated by structural factors such as income, education, political views, race and so on, but increasingly also by cultural practices. A division between liberal and alternative views, on the one hand, and traditional, anti-elitist and national views, on the other

© The Author(s) 2022, corrected publication 2023
R. Heikkilä, *Understanding Cultural Non-Participation in an Egalitarian Context*, Palgrave Studies in Cultural Participation,
https://doi.org/10.1007/978-3-031-18865-7_1

hand, seems to be capturing peoples' political and value orientations better than the traditional left-right scale (Flanagan and Lee 2003; Hooghe
et al. 2002). In this scenario, high culture has been increasingly positioned
as an 'elitist' pursuit. This label is at least partly true in the sense that
according to most scholarly research on the topic, many people seem to be
'non-participants' when it comes to culture. This scenario looked to me
like an enigma when I first came across it. What were all these people with
supposedly zero interest in cultural participation doing? Were they all similar? And why did they refrain from participation—for practical, social or
political reasons? If, for instance, museums were technically open to everyone, what was the strong social force that made some people exclude
themselves? These questions intrigued me when I first started working on
my PhD in 2006 as part of a research project on cultural capital and social
stratification in Finland (Rahkonen et al. 2006), which was intended as the
Finnish counterpart to the UK's Cultural Capital and Social Exclusion
study (Bennett et al. 2009).

Of course, the first evident finding in all cross-cultural research was that
cultural participation was socially structured and that culturally active people were better off, while non-participants were linked to low positions in
society. Cultural participation thus seemed to be essentially a question of
inequality. At the same time, the booming 'everyday participation' debate
started to emphasise the more mundane pastimes of the working and
lower classes (Miles and Gibson 2016). Still, I noticed early in my own
research that people with lower cultural participation answered various
surveys much less willingly than culturally active people and were more
reluctant participants in the follow-up interviews that I was conducting for
the research project. Therefore, studying cultural practices, specifically
participation, seemed to run the risk of producing a skewed image in
favour of the people who were engaged participants while revealing barely
anything about the people who participated very little.

With this dilemma in mind, I applied for funding for a research project
titled Understanding Cultural Disengagement in Contemporary Finland.
The project received funding and started in 2017. I wanted to thoroughly
understand what cultural non-participation really meant and whether it
actually existed. My aim was to find out what the leisure of the supposedly
disengaged people looked like and how they reacted to the normative
demand that everyone 'should' participate. To achieve my purpose, I

talked about cultural practices and everyday life with 40 different individuals and nine focus groups in Finland whose backgrounds matched, according to previous research, the known background factors associated with low cultural participation—mainly having low education, living in a small place, working in a manual job, living in remote areas and so on. On the whole, my interviewees were people with common educational trajectories, mainstream jobs and typical family structures for Finnish lower or popular classes (cf. Purhonen et al. 2014): 'common people' rather than an excluded and marginalised minority. My research questions needed to be investigated in light of their empirical context, Finland—an egalitarian country with relatively equal possibilities for cultural participation and supposedly few lifestyle distinctions. Therefore, I decided to include the idea of egalitarianism in the book, beginning with its title.

It has been claimed that cultural participation, as a structure that brings strangers together for something that occurs in the public sphere, is central to the definition of the modern public mindset (Sennett 2002). Moreover, in recent years, cultural participation has become a hot topic in the sociology of culture (Gayo 2017; Reeves and de Vries 2019; Willekens and Lievens 2016). At the same time, active cultural participation has been continuously linked to high education and class position across different national contexts (Bennett et al. 2009; Purhonen et al. 2014; Reeves and de Vries 2019). This disproportionality and social inequality in cultural participation is mirrored in cultural production (Brook et al. 2020) and is further reflected in the discourse of cultural non-participation as a challenge or a problem (Balling and Kann-Christenssen 2013; Stevenson et al. 2017; Stevenson 2013), which often leads to the stigmatisation of non-participants as deviants (Stevenson 2019).

A highly important recent turn in the cultural participation debate has involved the idea that the *volume* of cultural participation could be a more important structuring factor regarding participation than the traditional divide between 'high' and 'low' culture (Prieur and Savage 2013; Purhonen et al. 2014; Savage et al. 2015; Weingartner and Rössel 2019). A 'voracious' or insatiable cultural participant is a product of modern capitalism: busy, harried and multitasking, within and beyond cultural participation (Ollivier 2008; Sullivan and Katz-Gerro 2007). The growing importance of the activity dimension has largely been seen as part of the transformation towards post-materialism and self-expression, which entails a higher tolerance towards other cultures and thus less need for highbrow snobbery (Weingartner and Rössel 2019). At the same time, it echoes the arguments that the distinctiveness of highbrow cultural practices would be diminishing (Lareau and Weininger 2003).

But what exactly is participation, anyway? The Oxford English Dictionary defines it as follows: 'The process or fact of sharing in an action, sentiment, etc.; (now esp.) active involvement in a matter or event, esp. one in which the outcome directly affects those taking part'. Attending a concert, playing an instrument or singing in a choir are at the core of different definitions of participation, as we shall see. Helping neighbours, joining an association, going to the gym, collecting coins or watching television are categorised as participation according to the broader understandings of 'everyday participation'. However, should minding your cat, looking for different puzzles on the internet, finding used parts for broken motorcycles or having sex also be categorised as participation? These are all leisure pursuits and very common ones. But are they really part of 'sharing in an action' or 'active involvement'? In addition, their 'problem' in being recognised as cultural participation is that they are situated extremely far from legitimised, canonised participatory practices. And yet, such activities constitute the everyday practices of many ordinary people: in fact, they all were mentioned by one or several of my interviewees.

THEORETICAL AND METHODOLOGICAL STARTING POINTS

This book builds on the theoretical framework of French sociologist Pierre Bourdieu and his idea that lifestyles are homologous to the surrounding social structures. According to this thesis, cultural practices—understood as taste, knowledge and participation—correspond to the social class structure according to existing hierarchies: upper classes practice culture that is considered 'higher', and the lower classes practice culture considered 'lower'. This leads to what Bourdieu calls distinction (Bourdieu 1984/1979). In his theory, when it comes to lifestyle, power relations work in a way in which hierarchically higher cultural practices are assigned more value than lower ones—the former are granted *legitimacy* and enjoy an undisputed taken-for-grantedness. Whereas the upper classes, according to Bourdieu, exhibit an 'aesthetic disposition', or a capacity to prioritise form over function and make 'disinterested' judgements on culture, the lower classes conceive culture through an attitude of functional 'popular aesthetic' (Bourdieu 1984/1979). The cultural practices of the privileged classes appear 'highbrow' and legitimate in the eyes of the other classes, which usually either strive for equality without ever really succeeding—for example, with the middle classes attempting to nudge their children into prestigious cultural hobbies—or adopt practically oriented tastes because nothing else is available to them, as the working classes do by watching TV or sneering at opera-goers. This latter claim regarding the 'taste of necessity' that Bourdieu ascribes to the working classes has been widely criticised (see Bennett 2011 and Chap. 4). Cultural practices may seem like aleatory personal choices, but in Bourdieu's theory, they become vehicles of violence that separate 'legitimate' from 'illegitimate' cultural practices in practically all fields of culture. Different cultural practices are thus seen as a 'socially innocent language of likes and dislikes' (Bourdieu 1984/1979, 239) that makes them misrecognised as markers of class hierarchies and inequality.

This means that cultural non-participation can also very quickly elicit labels such as narrow-mindedness and lack of knowledge (Stevenson 2019). When taken into account that active cultural participation is linked to high-status qualities, such as high education, high income and so on (Heikkilä and Lindblom 2022; Reeves and de Vries 2019), this scenario almost by default paves the way for a denigration of cultural non-participation as a feature of the lower classes, seen not only as 'ignorant' or 'vulgar' (Bourdieu 1984/1979) but also as unwillingness to learn by participating in culture (Stevenson 2019). McKenzie (2015) argued that the working classes are seen as 'unidimensional' and lacking 'positive namings and valuations'; this becomes very clear through the use of pejorative labels, such as 'chavs' (Jones 2016) or 'underclasses' (Tyler 2013). Finally, regarding the judgements received by the working classes, it has been claimed that the lower classes have the tools and resources to reject these unjustifiable and undesired judgements (Skeggs and Loveday 2012). The question of how exactly this rejection occurs in an egalitarian country such as Finland will be one of the key themes of this book.

Bourdieu's theory has been fundamentally questioned over the years, although it should be remembered that his empirical data and approach were deeply embedded in the cultural and ideological context of 1960s France, a very different world from today's post-consumerist and relatively individualistic Western societies. Yet, this book takes the critiques and updates on Bourdieu's work very seriously indeed—and tries to work beyond them. According to one of the most important critical arguments against Bourdieu, modern consumer-citizens live in rapidly transforming societies with plenty of room for leading individualistic lifestyles free from class constraints and sensitive to peers, life-courses and significant others

(Featherstone 1991; Lahire 2004). In the last 30 years or so, the 'omnivore debate' has questioned whether highbrow snobbery actually functions as a sign of cultural distinction or whether previous highbrow snobs are starting to participate in both highbrow and popular culture (Peterson 2005). Finally, scholars have wondered what really works as effective cultural capital in different contexts—for example, what forms of cultural participation are strong enough to create social exclusions or to form difficult-to-cross group boundaries? Lamont and Lareau argued that 'the power exercised through cultural capital … is first and foremost a power to shape other people's lives through exclusion and symbolic imposition' (1988, 159). This means that classical highbrow culture is not linked to cultural capital as such; rather, national contexts and the institutionalisation of certain kinds of cultural practices grant cultural capital to certain forms of cultural participation. Within the scope of this book, it is especially interesting to consider what works (or not) as cultural capital among Finnish underprivileged groups.

Finally, Michèle Lamont's important criticism of Bourdieu's model was that the latter exaggerated the importance of cultural and economic resources and overlooked the significance of morality. Lamont created the concept of symbolic boundaries to mark the conceptual distinctions or rules used to 'categorise objects, people, practices' and to 'separate people into groups' (Lamont and Molnár 2002, 168), which helped understand how people regarded those above and below them in hierarchies. Lamont also distinguished between cultural, economic and moral symbolic boundaries. In her comparative study between French and North American upper-class men, Lamont found that the cultural context was essential for boundary-drawing: whereas cultural boundaries were central in France, in the USA cultural boundaries were much looser, with more emphasis being placed on moral boundaries. However, the symbolic boundary approach has been strongly criticised because of its tendency to separate boundary types—for instance, Jarness and Flemmen (2019) argued that moral boundaries work very differently when drawn upwards or downwards and that boundaries very rarely exist in their 'pure' form.

AIMS AND DEFINITIONS

The aim of this book is to provide a systematic understanding of cultural non-participation in contemporary Finland. My research was centred on two fundamental research questions:

1. How is the cultural participation of the hypothetically 'non-participating' groups constituted in Finland?
2. What kinds of boundaries do they draw while talking about their cultural participation?

In order to be able to these questions, I will next define the main concepts used in the book.

We have already used a dictionary definition of 'participation', but defining 'cultural participation' is a more difficult task. The different operationalisations of cultural participation are thoroughly discussed in Chap. 3; we will see that different scholars have operationalised cultural participation in highly diverse ways. Moreover, there is no established system of categorising the different forms of cultural participation: while many scholars follow the Bourdieusian way of coupling directly highbrow cultural practices with the culture of high-status groups, for instance, Warde and Gayo-Cal (2009) have suggested a more fixed conceptualization of cultural practices, using education as a proxy to distinguish between the cultural practices of highly educated groups compared to those without educational qualifications (arriving at a tripartite division between highbrow, common and unauthorised cultural practices).

In this book, after finding that cultural participation was described on many different levels by my interviewees, I have decided to speak about *highbrow-oriented*, *popular* and *everyday* cultural participation. By highbrow-oriented cultural participation, I refer to canonical cultural practices, such as attending the opera, ballet or theatre, going to museums, reading books, listening to classical music and so on, which are linked to the cultural practices of high-status groups (Reeves and de Vries 2019), also in Finland (Purhonen et al. 2011, 2014). Popular culture is usually understood as a simple counterpart of 'highbrow' taste (thus 'lowbrow'), something for which Bourdieu has been criticised—for instance, by Fiske (1987/2010)—because popular culture clearly includes meaning-making and a certain accumulation of capital just like highbrow-oriented culture. By popular cultural participation, I refer to common cultural practices, such as going to the cinema, watching TV, attending the circus, going to a pop or folk concert or listening to similar music at home, which are linked to how previous studies have conceptualised popular culture (Gayo 2017; Katz-Gerro and Jaeger 2013; Warde et al. 2007). Finally, everyday participation refers to a more recent debate that starts with the mundane and community-centred everyday leisure practices that were previously not even considered when studying cultural participation (Ebrey 2016; Miles and Gibson 2016). Following other studies (Leguina and Miles 2017; Miles and Sullivan 2012), I take everyday cultural participation to involve mundane and informal activities, such as doing crosswords, social-ising with relatives, walking the dog, attending fairs or flea markets and so on. Faced with a large number of different terms for capturing non-participation in culture (e.g. cultural disengagement, passivity, inactivity and so on; see Chap. 3 for an in-depth discussion), I have chosen to use the least normative and hopefully the most neutral term, namely *non-participation*, when describing the simple lack of participation in either highbrow-oriented, popular or everyday culture.

A significant empirical question looms over the discussion: How do these three different forms of cultural participation relate to *cultural capital*? Bourdieu's theory is based on the assumption that the social classes—the upper classes, the middle classes and the working, or popular, classes—have different amounts of resources, which he conceptualised as capitals: economic, cultural and social capital (Bourdieu 1986). Class, for Bourdieu, involves two dimensions: the overall volume of capitals and the composition of capitals. The higher the capital volumes, the higher people are in the social structure (Bourdieu 1984/1979). Many scholars have argued that the compositions of capitals are important in determining an individual's status in the social structure (Blasius and Friedrichs 2008). According to Bourdieu's theory, the three capitals are interchangeable: economic capital can be converted into cultural capital by, for example, buying a theatre ticket, cultural capital can be converted into social capital by using certain language skills to enter privileged groups, and social capital can be converted into economic capital by using one's connections to get a good job—and so on (cf. Reeves and de Vries 2019). Bourdieu reminds us, however, that this interchangeability is not automatic: espe-cially the realm of cultural production is an 'economic world reversed' in which economic capital, such as high sales numbers, becomes problematic in terms of the possible prestige and exclusivity of works of art (Bourdieu 1993).

Bourdieu originally coined the concept of cultural capital to explain the link between the academic success of educated parents' children. According to Bourdieu's argumentation, formal school curricula include items (e.g. highbrow arts) that are already familiar to children from educated families (Bourdieu and Passeron, 1979; DiMaggio, 1982; Lareau and Weininger, 2003). These children, then, are rewarded for their 'cultivated naturalness' (Bourdieu 1984/1979, 71), even if their skills are socially inherited and eventually embodied. Other scholars have pointed out that the value of cultural capital may be different from what Bourdieu originally meant. The debate has mainly been between 'fixed' and 'floating' concepts of cultural capital (cf. Prieur and Savage 2013). Lamont and Lareau proposed that cultural capital should refer to 'widely shared, high status cultural signals used for social and cultural exclusion' (1988, 156), allowing for a certain fluctuation of the value of different cultural products over time.

Finally, in addition to the concept of cultural capital, Bourdieu's concept of habitus may facilitate our understanding of why some people feel more at home than others when participating in certain forms of culture. According to Bourdieu, the durable and transposable habitus becomes 'second nature' as a set of class-based and embodied dispositions that help people navigate the social structure, giving them an idea of what kinds of cultural practices are possible for people like them (Bourdieu 1993). Habitus provides an individual with 'a sense of one's place which leads one to exclude oneself from places from which one is excluded' (Bourdieu 1984/1979, 471).

Mapping the Context

Some words should be said about the empirical context, namely, Finland. Finland is a Nordic country with a relatively small population of 5.5 million people. Although a Western capitalist economy, it is one of the countries scoring highest in egalitarian values and the redistribution of wealth, which makes Finland one of the so-called Nordic welfare states (Esping-Andersen 1999). Finland has a largely de-commodified public sector with, for instance, an almost completely public and free education system, including university studies. Taxation is relatively high; particularly income taxes are high compared to other countries (OECD 2022). Voter turnout is high compared to many other countries (OECD 2019). In terms of the labour market, Finland boasts a collective bargaining system and a permanently high trade union density compared to other European countries (Ruostetsaari 2015; Stokke and Thornqvist 2001). Economic, labour market and social policy debates have historically been marked by a will to reach consensus (Ruostetsaari 2015). A traditionally centralised model of industrial relations has only recently started to loosen up. Although Finland has a strong labour movement with historical roots, compared to

most other European countries, the country has experienced industrialisa-
tion and urbanisation relatively late, and a certain 'rural identity' is still
central for many people (Kantola et al. 2022). Finland is an EU member
since 1995 and is part of the EMU with Euro currency. At the time of
writing this book, Finland is applying for NATO membership together
with Sweden.

In terms of cultural sociology, Finnish sociologists have often claimed
that Finland lacks 'class culture' and, therefore, effective possibilities for
true lifestyle distinctions (Mäkelä 1985), mainly due to historical reasons,
such as a lack of a proper feudal nobility. These claims have been criticised
and even proved wrong; in fact, Finland has similar patterns of heavily
class-based lifestyles as do other countries in the Global North, and education functions as an important factor in structuring lifestyles (Heikkilä
2021; Purhonen et al. 2014). Recently, scholars have identified polarisation in many of the key institutions of egalitarian Finland. Regarding voter
turnout, recent research has revealed a trend of polarisation along socio-
economic lines (Lahtinen 2019). Regarding media repertoires, socioeco-
nomically underprivileged groups seem to be drifting towards increasingly
narrow and restricted media consumption habits (Heikkilä et al. 2020). In
a previously highly egalitarian setting of equal public education, there is
increasing segregation of schools (Bernelius and Vaattovaara 2016).

Despite these developments, Finland is still considered an egalitarian
country. In the Nordic countries, egalitarianism—often characterised
as a belief in human equality at the social, political and economic levels—has entailed a particular demand for anti-elitism: people generally
consider themselves equal in the Nordic countries, and there is, for
instance, a tendency to avoid titles or to downplay economic wealth
(Daloz 2007; Hjellbrekke et al. 2015; Skarpenes and Sakslind 2010).
In Nordic societies, groups occupying top positions in the social hierarchy have typically preferred to portray themselves as 'ordinary'
(Ljunggren 2017). In Finland, the elites have been keen to emphasise
their humility in a framework of modesty belonging to the Lutheran
tradition (Kantola and Kuusela 2019). Although factors such as relatively small income differences and equal education opportunities help
foster egalitarianism, they do not necessarily translate into equal cultural practices; on the contrary, such factors can conceal and even shape
hierarchical structures. As Jarness (2017, 369) argued, 'Egalitarianism
functions as a misrecognised counterforce members of the culturally
privileged middle class direct against members of the economically

privileged middle class – and vice versa' (see also Jarness 2015). De Keere (2020) found that support for egalitarianism is skewed towards groups with some cultural but little economic capital; their opposite is found in groups with little capitals in general but characterised by some economic capital—among them De Keere encountered a 'fatalistic' worldview which is characterised by distrust towards regulations and an idea that society is not trustworthy or even profitable. In Finland, concerns have arisen about different societal groups drifting further away from one another—for instance, in a large recent study, Kantola et al. (2022) found that Finns with very little income and precarious positions largely share a lack of confidence in the welfare state. In this light, although the topic of this book is cultural non-participation in general and not the Finnish case as such, Finland is an interesting context for studying this topic.

THE DESIGN OF THIS BOOK

This book consists of three parts. In the first part, 'Situating the Research', the Introduction is followed by three chapters that form the theoretical backbone of the work. Chapter 2 contextualises cultural participation by first discussing cultural participation as a positional good. Then, the chapter asks whether there can be a 'moral turn' in the cultural practices of different underprivileged groups. Finally, cultural policy is discussed as legitimation for certain kinds of cultural practices. Chapter 3 deals with cultural participation and non-participation in relation to the previous literature. The chapter discusses the connections between social status and cultural participation, followed by the many different definitions and operationalisations of cultural participation and non-participation. Finally, 'everyday participation' is discussed in a sub-chapter. Chapter 4 lays the groundwork for the subsequent empirical chapters. It contains a description of the challenges involved in studying the cultural non-participation of underprivileged groups and offers details about my data collection process, the data themselves and the analysis. The second part of the book, 'Cultural Milieus of the Potentially Passive', presents the empirical material. This part is divided into three chapters according to the interviewees' main discourses regarding cultural participation: 'affirmation', 'functionality' and 'resistance'. I did not group the interviewees according to these categories; rather, I identified the major discourses employed by the interviewees themselves. In addition to standard excerpts from interviews, the chapters contain illustrative text boxes focusing on individual empirical cases that help clarify key theoretical concepts or ideas. The last part, 'Paving the Way for Future Debates', contains the concluding chapter. It provides an overview of how cultural non-participation should and could be understood in the highly egalitarian context of Finland. It also deals with the often-problematic role of cultural policy in trying to alter existing hierarchies. After discussing the limitations of my study, the chapter outlines an agenda for future research.

Finally, some reflections on interview dynamics are in order. My role as the interviewer certainly affected both the interview situations and their analytical outcomes. Qualitative interviews are typically asymmetrical in terms of power dynamics because interview situations are usually dominated by the interviewer (Bengtsson and Fynbo 2018). At the time of the interviews, I was an academic woman in my mid-thirties with prestigious state funding, and I was consciously recruiting interviewees with background factors predicting low cultural participation (see Chap. 4). The combination of my age, gender and education may have seemed surprising, ridiculous or even provocative to some interviewees, and in one way or another, this situation was often referred to in the interviews themselves (for a more detailed account, see Heikkilä and Katainen 2021). A particular sensitivity was often needed on my part; as Michèle Lamont did during her interviews with French and North American upper-class men, I attempted to 'minimize distorting effects' (Lamont 1992, 19) by presenting myself as a harmless, non-intrusive and non-judgemental outsider to the interviewees' many different cultural and geographical contexts in order to put them at ease and encourage them to speak. Much like Justin Gest, who recently studied working-class culture in the USA and the UK, I also made every effort to attain 'full immersion into communities' (Gest 2016, 206), often spending many days in the towns in which I conducted interviews, getting to know and better understand my interviewees and their local contexts. In this sense, qualitative methods proved to be an effective means of gaining at least some access to difficult-to-reach profiles. My wish is to have captured the 'seemingly unimportant' (Back 2015) aspects of the daily lives of my interviewees; the following chapters will show whether I have succeeded in this task.

REFERENCES

Back L (2015) Why Everyday Life Matters: Class, Community and Making Life Livable. *Sociology* 49(5): 820–836.

Balling G and Kann-Christenssen N (2013) What is a non-user? An analysis of Danish surveys on cultural habits and participation. *Cultural Trends* 22(2): 67–76.

Bengtsson TT and Fynbo L (2018) Analysing the significance of silence in qualitative interviewing: Questioning and shifting power relations. *Qualitative Research* 18(1): 19–35.

Bennett T, Savage M, Silva E, Warde A, Gayo-Cal M and Wright D (2009) *Culture, Class, Distinction*. London: Routledge.

Bennett T (2011) Culture, choice, necessity: A political critique of Bourdieu's aesthetic. *Poetics* 39: 530–546.

Bennett T (1995) *The Birth of the Museum. History, Theory, Politics*. London: Routledge.

Bernelius V and Vaattovaara M (2016) Choice and segregation in the 'most egalitarian' schools: Cumulative decline in urban schools and neighbourhoods of Helsinki, Finland. *Urban Studies* 53(15): 3155–3171.

Blasius J and Friedrichs J (2008) Lifestyles in distressed neighborhoods: A test of Bourdieu's "taste of necessity" hypothesis. *Poetics* 36(1): 24–44.

Bourdieu P (1993) *The Field of Cultural Production. Essays on Art and Literature*. New York: Columbia Press.

Bourdieu P (1984/1979) *Distinction. A Social Critique of the Judgment of Taste*. London: Routledge & Kegan Paul.

Bourdieu P (1986) The Forms of Capital. In J. Richardson (Ed.), *Handbook of Theory and Research for the Sociology of Education* (pp. 241–258). New York: Greenwood.

Bourdieu P and Passeron JC (1979) *The Inheritors: French Students and Their Relation to Culture*. Chicago, IL: University of Chicago Press.

Brook O, O'Brien D and Taylor M (2020) *Culture is Bad for You*. Manchester: Manchester University Press.

Daloz JP (2007) Elite distinction: grand theory and comparative perspectives. *Comparative Sociology* 6(1–2): 27–74.

De Keere K (2020) Finding the moral space: Rethinking morality, social class and worldviews. *Poetics* 79: 101415.

Di Maggio P (1982) Cultural capital and school success: the impact of status culture participation on the grades of United States high-school students. *American Sociological Review* 47: 189–201.

Ebrey J (2016) The mundane and insignificant, the ordinary and the extraordinary: Understanding Everyday Participation and theories of everyday life. *Cultural Trends* 25(3): 158–168.

Esping-Andersen G (1999) *Social Foundations of Postindustrial Economies.* Oxford: Oxford University Press.

Featherstone M (1991) *Consumer culture and postmodernism.* London: Sage.

Fiske J (1987/2010) *Television culture.* London: Routledge.

Flanagan S C and Lee AR (2003) The New Politics, Culture Wars, and The Authoritarian- Libertarian Value Change in Advanced Industrial Democracies. *Comparative Political Studies* 36(3): 235–270.

Gayo M (2017) Exploring Cultural Disengagement: The Example of Chile. *Cultural Sociology* 11(4): 468–488.

Gest J (2016). *The new minority. White working class politics in an age of immigration and inequality.* Oxford: Oxford University Press.

Heikkilä R (2021) The slippery slope of cultural non-participation: Orientations of participation among the potentially passive. *European Journal of Cultural Studies* 24: 202–219.

Heikkilä R and Katainen A (2021) Counter-talk as symbolic boundary drawing: Challenging legitimate cultural practices in individual and focus group interviews in the lower regions of social space. *Sociological Review* 69: 1029–1050.

Heikkilä R and Lindblom T (2022) Overlaps and accumulations: The anatomy of cultural non-participation in Finland, 2007 to 2018. *Journal of Consumer Culture.* Available at: https://doi.org/10.1177/14695405211062052 (Accessed 21 August 2022).

Heikkilä R, Leguina A and Purhonen S (2020) The stratification of media usage in Finland, 2007–2018: Signs of socio-political polarization? *New Media & Society* 24(5): 1053–1075.

Hjellbrekke J, Jarness V, Korsnes O (2015) Cultural distinctions in an 'egalitarian' society. In: Coulangeon P and Duval J (eds) *The Routledge Companion to Bourdieu's Distinction.* Oxon: Routledge, pp. 187–206.

Hooghe L, Marks G and Wilson CJ (2002) Does Left/Right Structure Party Positions on European Integration? *Comparative Political Studies* 35(8): 965–989.

Jarness V (2015) Modes of consumption: From 'what' to 'how' in cultural stratification research. *Poetics* 53: 65–79.

Jarness V (2017) Cultural vs Economic Capital: Symbolic Boundaries within the Middle Class. *Sociology* 51(2): 357–373.

Jarness V and Flemmen M (2019) A struggle on two fronts: Boundary drawing in the lower region of the social space and the symbolic market for "down-to-earthness". *British Journal of Sociology* 70: 166–189.

Jones O (2016) *Chavs. The demonization of the working class.* London: Verso.

Kantola A, Aaltonen S, Haikkola L, Junnilainen L, Luhtakallio E, Patana P, Timonen J and Tuominen P (2022) *Kahdeksan kuplan Suomi. Yhteiskunnan muutosten syvät tarinat [Finland's eight bubbles. The deep stories of societal changes]*. Gaudeamus: Helsinki.

Kantola A and Kuusela H (2019) Wealth Elite Moralities: Wealthy Entrepreneurs' Moral Boundaries. *Sociology* 53(2): 368–384.

Katz-Gerro T and Jaeger MM (2013) Top of the pops, ascend of the omnivores, defeat of the couch potatoes: Cultural consumption profiles in Denmark 1975–2004. *European Sociological Review* 29(2): 243–260.

Mc Kenzie L (2015) *Getting By. Estates, Class and Culture in Austerity Britain*. London: Policy Press.

Lahire B (2004) *La Culture des individus. Dissonances culturelles et distinction de soi*. Paris: La Découverte.

Lahtinen H (2019) Socioeconomic differences in electoral participation – Insights from the Finnish administrative registers. Helsinki: Helsingin yliopisto.

Lamont M (1992) *Money, Morals and Manners: The Culture of the French and American Upper Middle Classes*. Chicago: University of Chicago Press.

Lamont M and Lareau A (1988) Cultural capital: Allusions, gaps and glissandos in recent theoretical developments. *Sociological theory* 153–168.

Lamont M and Molnár V (2002) The study of boundaries in the social sciences. *Annual Review of Sociology* 28: 167–195.

Lareau A and Weininger E B (2003) Cultural capital in educational research: A critical assessment. *Theory and Society* 32: 567–606.

Leguina A and Miles A (2017) Fields of participation and lifestyle in England: revealing the regional dimension from a reanalysis of the Taking Part Survey using Multiple Factor Analysis. *Cultural Trends* 26(1): 4–17.

Ljunggren J (2017) Elitist egalitarianism: Negotiating identity in the Norwegian cultural elite. *Sociology* 51(3): 559–574.

Miles A and Gibson L (2016) Everyday participation and cultural value. *Cultural Trends* 25(3): 151–157.

Miles A and Sullivan A (2012) Understanding participation in culture and sport: Mixing methods, reordering knowledges. *Cultural Trends* 21(4): 311–324.

Mäkelä K (1985) Kulttuurisen muuntelun yhteisöllinen rakenne Suomessa. *Sosiologia* 22(4): 247–260.

OECD (2022) Tax on personal income (indicator). Available at: https://doi.org/10.1787/94af18d7-en (Accessed 21 August 2022).

OECD (2019) "Voting". In: *Society at a Glance 2019: OECD Social Indicators*. Paris: OECD Publishing. OECD Publishing. Available at: https://doi.org/10.1787/3483a69a-en (Accessed 21 August 2022).

Ollivier M (2008) Modes of openness to cultural diversity. Humanist, populist, practical, and indifferent. *Poetics* 36 (2–3): 120–147.

Peterson RA (2005) Problems in comparative research: the example of omnivorousness. *Poetics* 33(5–6): 257–282.

Prieur A and Savage M (2013) Emerging forms of cultural capital. *European Societies* 15(2): 246–267.

Purhonen S, Gronow J and Rahkonen K (2011) Highbrow culture in Finland: Knowledge, taste and participation. *Acta Sociologica* 54(4): 385–402.

Purhonen S, Gronow J, Heikkilä R, Kahma N, Rahkonen K and Toikka A (2014) *Suomalainen maku: Kulttuuripääoma, kulutus ja elämäntyylien sosiaalinen eriytyminen [Finnish taste: Cultural capital, consumption and the social differentiation of lifestyles]*. Helsinki: Gaudeamus.

Rahkonen K, Haatanen K, Purhonen S, Kahma N and Heikkilä R (2006) Cultural Capital and Social Differentiation in Contemporary Finland: An International Comparison. Unpublished research plan.

Reeves A and de Vries R (2019) Can cultural consumption increase future earnings? Exploring the economic returns to cultural capital. *British Journal of Sociology* 70: 214–240.

Ruostetsaari I (2015) *Elite recruitment and coherence of the inner core of power in Finland: changing patterns during the economic crises of 1991–2011*. Lanham: Lexington Books.

Savage M, Cunningham N, Devine F, Friedman S, Laurison D, McKenzie L, Miles A, Snee H and Wakeling P (2015) *Social Class in the 21st Century*. London: Pelican.

Sennett R (2002) *The Fall of Public Man*. London: Penguin.

Skarpenes O, Sakslind R (2010) Education and egalitarianism: The culture of the Norwegian middle class. *The Sociological Review* 58(2): 219–245.

Skeggs B and Loveday V (2012) Struggles for Value: Value Practices, Injustice, Judgment, Affect and the Idea of Class. *The British Journal of Sociology* 63(3): 472–490.

Stevenson D (2019) The cultural non-participant: Critical logics and discursive subject identities. *Arts and the Market* 9(1): 50–64.

Stevenson D (2013) What's the problem again? The problematisation of cultural participation in Scottish cultural policy. *Cultural Trends* 22(2): 77–85.

Stevenson D, Balling G and Kann-Rasmussen N (2017) Cultural Participation in Europe: Shared Problem or Shared Problematisation? *International Journal of Cultural Policy* 23(1): 89–106.

Stokke TA and Thornqvist C (2001) Strikes and Collective Bargaining in the Nordic Countries. *European Journal of Industrial Relations* 7(3): 245–267.

Sullivan O and Katz-Gerro T (2007) The Omnivore Thesis Revisited: Voracious Cultural Consumers. European Sociological Review 23(2): 123–137.

Tyler I (2013) *Revolting Subjects: Social Abjection and Resistance in Neoliberal Britain.* London: Zed Books.

Warde A and Gayo-Cal M (2009) The anatomy of cultural omnivorousness: The case of the United Kingdom. *Poetics* 37: 119–145.

Warde A, Wright D and Gayo-Cal M (2007) Understanding Cultural Omnivorousness: Or, the Myth of the Cultural Omnivore. *Cultural Sociology* 1(2): 143–164.

Weingartner S and Rössel J (2019) Changing dimensions of cultural consumption? The space of lifestyles in Switzerland from 1976 to 2013. *Poetics* 74: 101345.

Willekens M and Lievens J (2016) Who participates and how much? Explaining non-attendance and the frequency of attending arts and heritage activities. *Poetics* 56: 50–63.

CHAPTER 2

Contextualising Cultural Participation

Abstract This chapter contextualises cultural participation as one of the three dimensions of cultural practices. It first discusses cultural participation as a positional good and as a vehicle of social exclusion. The chapter then introduces some of the main contributions arguing that the highbrow-oriented culture could be losing its distinctive value—most importantly, the discussions on the 'rise of the omnivore' and the 'meltdown scenario'. This chapter also summarises the research on the cultural practices of different underprivileged classes. It is argued that moral boundaries are an important means for underprivileged classes to defend their worth in a scenario of 'lacking' cultural or economic resources. Finally, this chapter shows that public cultural policy serves as an important tool for validating specific kinds of cultural participation.

Keywords Cultural participation • Cultural exclusion • Moral turn • Worth • Omnivorousness

CULTURAL PARTICIPATION AS A POSITIONAL GOOD

The social and hierarchical aspects of cultural participation have been the foci of key debates in cultural sociology since Bourdieu (1984/1979). As we saw in the Introduction, cultural participation is, together with cultural taste and knowledge, one of the three pillars of cultural practices. When studied separately from other types of cultural practices, cultural participation shows largely similar trends and hierarchical patterns of cultural stratification as cultural taste and knowledge. As we shall see in the following chapters, people with privileged backgrounds exhibit very different cultural participation patterns than their less privileged counterparts (Bennett et al. 2009; Heikkilä and Lindblom 2022; Purhonen et al. 2011). Bourdieu's original postulate, which received significant criticism later on, was the existence of a homology between class positions and lifestyle differences, which translates into social exclusion and an unequal distribution of opportunities. This, in turn, was said to create cultural stratification whereby privileged classes adopt 'highbrow' cultural practices to distinguish themselves from the lower groups (Bourdieu 1984/1979). Thus, cultural participation such as attending ballet or reading poetry becomes 'highbrow', while cultural participation such as attending a boxing match or baking bread at home becomes 'popular' or 'everyday' participation. A classic example of the privileged status of highbrow participation and highbrow art is their inclusion in school curricula: schools reward children from privileged backgrounds as naturally talented, even though their skills are actually a by-product of socially inherited cultivation (Bourdieu and Passeron 1979; DiMaggio 1982; Lareau and Weininger 2003).

What does the traditionally privileged status of highbrow culture imply for the social value attached to cultural participation? Although the debates on the value and eventual 'impact' of cultural participation have been going on since Antiquity (Belfiore and Bennett 2008), the most important contemporary reflections include the so-called meltdown scenario (DiMaggio and Mukhtar 2004) and the rise of the omnivore (Peterson and Kern 1996; Peterson and Simkus 1992). According to the meltdown scenario, the distinctive value of highbrow cultural participation is declining and losing its important function as a conveyor of cultural capital. This trend is said to be caused by significant devaluation of highbrow-oriented cultural participation, especially among women, the highly educated and the young, which leads to the ageing of the remaining highbrow participants. Nevertheless, DiMaggio and Mukhtar's (2004) original study assessing the 'meltdown' in the USA between 1982 and 2002 is not a straightforward confirmation of this scenario. Subsequent studies have shown that although there is evidence of decline in highbrow cultural participation in many national contexts, its association with cultural capital (instead of economic capital) remains largely intact (Yuksek et al. 2019).

Meanwhile, the debate on the 'rise of the omnivore' has claimed that a growing group of highly educated people who used to be 'snobs' is becoming more open, eclectic and tolerant in its cultural practices; by combining practices from both highbrow and popular cultural milieus, this group supposedly creates 'omnivorous' patterns of cultural practices for the higher status groups (Peterson and Kern 1996; Peterson and Simkus 1992). The theory of omnivorousness has cast doubts on Bourdieu's original thesis regarding the distinctiveness of highbrow cultural practices—for instance, Coulangeon and Lemel (2007, 94) stated that this theory can be directly 'interpreted as an invalidation of Bourdieu's sociology of taste'. At the same time, Lizardo and Skiles (2012) argued that omnivorousness is compatible with Bourdieu's theory and interpreted omnivorous cultural practices as a form of Bourdieusian aesthetic dispositions that can be converted into cultural capital. The original claim of 'rising omnivorousness' has received mild support but also ample criticism, especially regarding the possibility that omnivorousness may be a methodological artefact (Brisson 2019; see also Peterson 2005). Recent research has suggested that the most omnivorous cultural practices could actually be found among middle-status groups rather than among high-status groups (Nault et al. 2021).

What has happened, then, to the long-standing trends of highbrow-oriented cultural participation? According to many sources, participation in highbrow activities has remained stable over recent decades (DiMaggio and Mukhtar 2004; Roose and Daenekindt 2015). Highbrow art still receives ample funding throughout the Global North (Council of Europe 2021; Heilbrun and Gray 2001; Saukkonen 2014). Highbrow cultural practices have retained their place in school curricula (Daenekindt and Roose 2015). However, from the perspective of cultural production, a previously tightly defined and narrow sphere of highbrow art does seem to be opening up to increased cultural heterogeneity in a double process of the legitimisation of popular culture and the popularisation of traditional legitimate culture (Purhonen et al. 2019). Still, there are no univocal signals or trends to suggest that the privileged status of highbrow-oriented cultural practices would be dissolving (Daenekindt and Roose 2015).

Along the lines of the omnivorousness debate, with high-status groups supposedly adopting broadly 'omnivorous' cultural practices, low-status groups have been seen as the logical opposite: a group defined mostly by its cultural exclusion (Peterson 1992). In other words, if the breadth of cultural practices indicates high-status distinction, lower taste groups are left with narrow cultural practices characterised by high volumes of dislikes and non-participation (Bryson 1997; 1996; Heikkilä and Lindblom 2022). Although these narrow cultural practices were originally described as 'univorous' in contrast to the broadly 'omnivorous' taste, subsequent research has shown that the omnivore–univore argument does not apply to all fields of cultural practices (Chan and Goldthorpe 2007) and that univorous tastes could actually be linked to upper-middle and middle-status groups rather than lower social classes (López Sintas and García Álvarez 2004).

Finally, Veblen's theory of the 'leisure class' offers a useful perspective on the status value of cultural participation. In the late nineteenth century, Veblen argued that, as a result of what he called the 'barbarian past', upper-class elites, with their ample resources and willingness to display their 'pecuniary superiority', tended to adopt economically unproductive leisure activities to distinguish themselves from the working majority (Veblen 1889/1953). From this angle, cultural participation can be considered a 'positional good'. Although Veblen's nineteenth-century elites had the economic means and willingness to 'afford a life of idleness' (Veblen 1889/1953, 46) in order to stand out from the working classes, contemporary capitalist upper and upper-middle classes seem to distinguish themselves through their long working hours, busy agendas and lack of leisure time. Time management and a constant busyness have become normal in middle-class families (Darrah 2007), and leisure itself has changed from simply relaxing to a quest of finding original, exciting and memorable choices (Keinan and Kivetz 2011). In contemporary Western middle and upper-middle-class circles, an active, occupied and overworked lifestyle has become a status symbol (Bellezza et al. 2017; Sullivan and Katz-Gerro 2007): a busy person possesses, already since childhood, the desirable characteristics of self-management, motivation and productivity, even during leisure (Lareau 2011). In an era characterised by demands for people to become self-sufficient 'entrepreneurial selves' (Du Gay 1996), what can be said about the context of the cultural participation of the underprivileged classes?

CULTURES OF THE UNDERPRIVILEGED CLASSES: A MORAL TURN?

With the rise of right-wing populism across the Global North, there has been plenty of scholarly interest in the cultural universes of the different underprivileged groups of society (Charlesworth 2000; Cherlin 2014; Gest 2016; Gidron and Hall 2017; Hochschild 2016; Jarness and Flemmen 2019; McKenzie 2015; Lamont 2000; Skarpenes 2021; Tyler 2013; Williams 2017). Many recent studies have identified both structural and emotional gaps between the perceived honourable and dignified past of the lower groups of the class structure and the downward mobility they are experiencing in the twenty-first century. For instance, in his 'testimony' on a de-industrialised working-class area in the UK, Charlesworth (2000) spoke about a 'dying way of life' of the working classes: milieus once marked by hard work, solid industry and strong social ties are now characterised by worsening labour conditions, vulnerability at work and a consequently weak attachment to future aspirations. A very similar image was drawn by Gest (2016), who argued, based on empirical data from the USA and the UK, that the radicalisation and political withdrawal of the white working classes can be understood in terms of deprivation or a perceived loss of power fuelled by increasing globalisation and weakening trade unions—a scenario in which the white working classes start to consider themselves 'minorities'. In her influential book on the 'deep stories' behind the rise of populist right-wing politics in the USA, Hochschild (2016) attempted to break the 'empathy wall' between the left-leaning academic sociology and the heartlands of the white conservative working-class America, concluding that the deep divide stems from feelings of betrayal and the perception that political authorities are to blame for economic decline as well as social and environmental problems.

How, then, are these debates related to cultural participation? Previous research suggests that people who identify as economically underprivileged typically feel culturally distant from dominant societal groups. Already in the 1940s, Genevieve Knupfer summarised that 'low status people' participate less in cultural and social life than 'high status people' and that economic underprivilege easily turns into a 'psychological underprivilege' or a lack of self-esteem which 'increases the willingness of the low status person to participate in many phases of our predominantly middle-class culture' (Knupfer 1947, 114). This phenomenon seems to be durable: the 'status effect', people's subjective understanding of the respect or recognition that they receive, is a powerful predictor of certain political behaviours (Gidron and Hall 2017)—for example, low subjective social status is clearly associated with support for right-wing populist parties. There is large variation inside the underprivileged classes, from politically engaged ones—either through traditional pro-system means or through anti-system activities, as Gest (2016) has shown—to largely indifferent or passive groups, also in the Nordic countries (Salo and Rydgren 2021). Scholars have often argued that the popular classes appear to lack a shared culture (Bennett et al. 2009) and that they are extremely divided in terms of income and consumption (Hugrée et al. 2020). By and large, it can be expected, following Skeggs (1997), that working-class people, or underprivileged groups in general, feel excluded from large institutional structures, such as the labour market and the education system, and therefore disidentify with class, even though their everyday lives and cultural practices are entirely 'classed'.

The scholarly consensus that the underprivileged classes have faced steep downward mobility in the last decades leading to feelings of cultural stigmatisation has produced debates on whether moral standards can work for the underprivileged groups as a kind of alternative currency in the face of diminishing economic and cultural resources (Jarness and Flemmen 2019; Lamont 2000). Lamont (2018, 424) has famously argued that 'neoliberal scripts feed growing recognition gaps'—in other words, differences are growing between various societal groups regarding perceived worthiness and cultural membership, with the lower classes seeing themselves as incapable of achieving the neoliberal ideals of socio-economic success, self-reliance and self-management, which makes them feel stigmatised and de-valued. Lamont has claimed that this scenario further narrows down the cultural membership of the most vulnerable groups of society.

There are echoes of these developments and debates in the Nordic context. Based on focus group and survey data from Denmark, Harrits and Pedersen (2019) showed that working classes use moral categorisations as a strategy of increasing their own value: moral categorisations can challenge economic and cultural inequalities by forming an alternative hierarchy upon which lower-placed groups in the hierarchy can base their value, thus potentially compensating for low socio-economic and cultural boundaries. Still, Harrits and Pedersen concluded that socio-economic boundaries are the strongest of all boundaries and that moral categorisations mainly serve to legitimise already existing status differences. Contrary to Harrits and Pedersen, Skarpenes (2021) argued, using qualitative interview data with members of the Norwegian working class regarding their symbolic boundaries, that the Norwegian working classes still firmly believe in the Nordic model with its large public sector, collective bargaining, wage equality and tripartite agreements between trade unions, employers' organisations and the national government. According to Skarpenes, members of the working class have a sense of ownership of this Nordic model and draw harsh symbolic boundaries against people and groups that do not accept the social responsibilities that belong to them.

On a slightly different note, Jarness and Flemmen (2019) showed, based on Norwegian interview data with people with low levels of cultural and economic capitals, that the concept of 'moral boundaries' entails a complex interconnection between upward and downward boundaries and can be used to both mock the most resourceful groups and exclude and denigrate those that are placed even lower on the social ladder. This clearly resembles Skeggs's (1997) famous description of how British working-class women distinguished themselves from the groups they perceived as lower in an attempt to maintain 'respectability'. Jarness and Flemmen (2019) also made an important contribution by revealing an oscillation between mostly male 'moral defiance' and mostly female 'cultural deference' (demonstrated many times in different national contexts as women's tendency to be closer than men to many forms of cultural engagement; cf. Christin 2012; Katz-Gerro and Jaeger 2015; Lizardo 2006; Purhonen et al. 2014) and speculating whether this difference could be understood as women misrecognising or extending social hierarchies.

An attitude of moral defiance among the lower echelons of society is not far from what Paul Willis famously characterised as 'caged resentment' (Willis 1977/2017, 120), a ridiculisation and outright rejection of the middle-class way of life and cultural practices by the working-class 'lads' he studied or what Hochschild (2016) described as feelings of resentment or betrayal among contemporary American white working classes. De Keere (2020) has recently studied moral positions as markers of class and found, using data from Flanders, that groups with low amounts of economic capital in particular exhibited a fatalistic worldview: ideals of anti-establishment and non-conformity as well as the idea of not properly benefitting from how society works. This echoes what Skeggs and Loveday (2012) characterised as the 'value struggles' that underprivileged groups have to confront in the face of a normative consensus that claims they are dysfunctional, antisocial, morally dubious and so on. Skeggs and Loveday concluded that the underprivileged classes are perfectly aware of the judgements and forms of exploitation coming from above.

We have seen that moral boundaries have been considered an important means for underprivileged classes to defend their worth in a scenario in which they 'lack' cultural and/or economic resources and that, at the same time, there seems to be resistance and defiance among the lower classes towards established middle-class norms and valuations, be they aesthetical or moral. In this context, it is intriguing to look at public cultural policy as an attempt to lower barriers and enable different societal groups to broadly participate in culture while supporting institutionalised and canonised forms of cultural participation.

CULTURAL POLICY AS A TOOL FOR LEGITIMISING CERTAIN FORMS OF CULTURAL PARTICIPATION

We have seen that there are many arguments and scholarly findings on feelings of cultural 'devaluation' among underprivileged classes (Charlesworth 2000; Gest 2016; Hochschild 2016), which have to bear many derogatory labels associated with them (Jones 2016; Skeggs and Loveday 2012; Tyler 2013). These findings go hand in hand with contemporary discussions on the 'cultural non-participant' in the field of cultural policy. In recent decades, concerns have emerged regarding an alleged decrease in cultural participation and a subsequent challenge regarding non-participation in culture, with non-participation being portrayed as a 'problem' that requires a 'solution' (Balling and Kann-Christensen 2013; Stevenson et al. 2017; Stevenson 2013, 2019). This 'deficit model of participation'—in which non-participation is seen, from the perspective of governmental actors, as a 'lack' (Miles and Sullivan 2012)—also implies that non-participants of highbrow culture constitute an excluded minority, a claim that is erroneous, as we shall see more in detail in the next chapters.

An important point in the debate on cultural non-participation was formulated by Stevenson (2013, 2019), who argued that instead of a 'problem' what actually exists is a 'problematization' that is tightly linked to hegemonic institutional discourses. Stevenson claimed that the 'cultural non-participant' is a superficially constructed discursive subject identity that essentially blames the non-participating people, framing them as deprived, deviant and in need of 'meaningful transformative experiences'

(Stevenson 2019, 53). These 'transformations' are presented as being possible through (highbrow-oriented) cultural participation. When interviewing experts working in or for cultural organisations receiving state funding, Stevenson encountered a double standard in the 'cultural non-participant' discourse: highly educated experts framed cultural non-participants as excluded people in need of 'life-changing experiences' while claiming the right to shun certain forms of culture because of their own high status (Stevenson 2019). What is more, the publicly expressed excessive worry over the 'problem' of cultural non-participation ends up ultimately legitimising the institutions and organisations that produce and provide access to highbrow culture (Jancovich and Bianchini 2013). Cultural non-participation is thus defined from a top-down highbrow-oriented perspective and becomes a 'problem' only when defined from above in the social hierarchy. These are essential points in the cultural non-participation debate.

Cultural policy research has seen many debates on the enormously complex relationship between cultural participation and power in society (Hadley and Belfiore 2018). On the one hand, the ideal and the great promise of public cultural policy is that—because participation in culture is often assumed to be connected to many positive things in life, from individual well-being to larger social integration (Milling 2019)—successful cultural policy should ease social hierarchies by funding culture consumed by low-placed groups in the hierarchy (Belfiore 2002), for instance, via street art projects or neighbourhood renewal programmes. These kinds of policies are supposed to directly benefit lower-status groups. On the other hand, it is recognised that public funding of culture may simply reproduce existing socio-economic hierarchies by subventing the cultural participation of resourceful groups already high in the hierarchy (Feder and Katz-Gerro 2012), for instance, by funding operas, symphonic orchestras and theatres, whose audiences have an overrepresentation of well-off groups. This view is corroborated by the fact that the lion's share of public funding for culture is usually directed towards a relatively small number of highbrow-oriented fields of culture, which is also true in Finland (Saukkonen 2014). In the same vein, scholars have debated whether different kinds of elite groups have too much power in designing policies about which types of cultural participation to support (Jancovich 2017). The cultural policy aspect brings along a question of fairness: Whose cultural participation is seen as relevant enough to fund? Is there a risk that popular, rich and vernacular forms of cultural participation go unfunded simply because they are not considered high enough in the hierarchy?

In recent decades, and in the wake of new public management policies, cultural policy has undergone new kinds of evaluations and performance assessments on whether implemented policies have been 'successful' enough, often based on idealised images of the 'transformative powers' of cultural participation (Belfiore and Bennett 2010). There have been debates on whether audited and measured cultural participation is becoming the sole indicator of the eventual 'success' of different cultural policies (Bunting et al. 2019). Already in the early twenty-first century, Belfiore predicted that instrumental cultural policy was here to stay (Belfiore 2002): the tax money spent on culture and the arts can be justified as an 'investment' if it entails positive social and societal impacts, such as easing social exclusion, typically by trying to lower the threshold of cultural participation for groups that participate very little (e.g. ethnic minorities, disabled people or otherwise socially very excluded groups) and thus supposedly activating the alleged 'non-participants of culture'. However, there is empirical evidence that the reality behind this idealisation is very different. For instance, research on participatory decision-making shows that people who typically become engaged through various participatory programmes are people who are already participating (Jancovich and Ejgod Hansen 2018). Overall, practical 'barriers', such as lack of time and money, only appear to prevent the cultural participation of the people who are already participating in culture; the real obstacles for cultural participation seem to reside much deeper in the social structure and be connected to very low levels of cultural and social capital (Willekens and Lievens 2016). This echoes the empirical findings of Heikkilä and Lindblom (2022): the real non-participants are the people who have drifted away from every possible kind of participation, including participation in everyday culture. All this means that different initiatives for lowering the threshold of cultural participation through lower prices or different community projects run the risk of remaining meagre intents to curb the real problems of social inequality.

CONCLUSION: CULTURAL PARTICIPATION AS A QUESTION OF 'DESERVINGNESS'

We have seen that participation in culture, especially in cultural fields considered 'highbrow', functions as a status symbol. Although there are signs of a weakening of highbrow culture as an indicator of privileged status (DiMaggio and Mukhtar 2004; Peterson and Kern 1996; Peterson and Simkus 1992), it can be argued that a hierarchy of lifestyles remains, with many studies arguing that different underprivileged groups feel isolated and de-valued, even culturally stigmatised (Charlesworth 2000; Gest 2016; Hochschild 2016; Lamont 2018; Skeggs and Loveday 2012). There is evidence that, due to their 'lack' of cultural resources, they mobilise different moral boundaries to express their own dignity and worth.

Finally, we have seen that it is debatable whether public cultural policy actually manages to improve access to culture or even lower much its barriers. Rather, it looks as if such policy serves as a tool for validating and legitimising specific kinds of highbrow-oriented cultural participation (Belfiore and Bennett 2007; Jancovich and Bianchini 2013) and represents, to a large extent, the interests of a narrow cultural elite (Jancovich 2017). In the same way, the discourse regarding the 'problem' of non-participation, which involves blaming and shaming non-participants, can be considered a handy means for arts organisations to legitimise the funding that they receive (Stevenson 2019). Considering that the bulk of public funding for culture and the arts is channelled mostly to highbrow culture, it is important to ask which segments of society receive the highest subventions for their forms of cultural participation and why.

There is thus a need to understand better how cultural non-participation should be conceptualised. According to Stevenson's argument, cultural non-participation is a label given from above to people and groups that stand out as problematic for other, mainly structural reasons (for instance, because of their poverty) that serve to categorise non-participants as narrow-minded and lacking knowledge or even willingness to learn. Thus, we end up with the notion of 'flawed subjectivities' (Stevenson 2019) whose contribution to any level of cultural participation is further diminished via this pejorative labelling. The next chapter on the existing scholarly literature on cultural participation and non-participation will help us contextualise this argument further.

REFERENCES

Balling G and Kann-Christenssen N (2013) What is a non-user? An analysis of Danish surveys on cultural habits and participation. *Cultural Trends* 22(2): 67–76.

Belfiore E (2002) Art as a means of alleviating social exclusion: Does it really work? A critique of instrumental cultural policies and social impact studies in the UK. *International Journal of Cultural Policy* 8(1): 91–106.

Belfiore E and Bennett O (2007) Rethinking the social impact of the arts. *International Journal of Cultural Policy* 13(2): 135–151.

Belfiore E and Bennett O (2008) *The social impact of the arts: an intellectual history*. Basingstoke: Palgrave.

Belfiore E and Bennett O (2010) Beyond the "Toolkit Approach": Arts Impact Evaluation Research and the Realities of Cultural Policy-Making. *Journal for Cultural Research* 14(2): 121–142.

Bellezza S, Paharia N, Keinan A (2017) Conspicuous Consumption of Time: When Busyness and Lack of Leisure Time Become a Status Symbol. *Journal of Consumer Research* 44(1): 118–138.

Bennett T, Savage M, Silva E, Warde A, Gayo-Cal M and Wright D (2009) *Culture, Class, Distinction*. London: Routledge.

Bourdieu P (1984/1979) *Distinction. A Social Critique of the Judgment of Taste*. London: Routledge & Kegan Paul.

Bourdieu P and Passeron JC (1979) *The Inheritors: French Students and Their Relation to Culture*. Chicago, IL: University of Chicago Press.

Brisson R (2019) Back to the original omnivore: on the artefactual nature of Peterson's thesis of omnivorousness. *Poetics* 76: 101359.

Bryson B (1997) What about the univores? Musical dislikes and group-based identity construction among Americans with low levels of education. *Poetics* 25 (2–3): 141–156.

Bryson B (1996) Anything but Heavy Metal: Symbolic exclusion and musical dislikes. *American Sociological Review* 61(5): 884–899.

Bunting C, Gilmore A and Miles A (2019) Calling participation to account: Taking part in the politics of method. In Belfiore E and Gibson L (eds) *Histories of Cultural Participation, Values and Governance*. London: Palgrave, pp. 183–210.

Chan TW and Goldthorpe JH (2007) Social stratification and cultural consumption: The visual arts in England. *Poetics* 35 (2–3): 168–190.

Charlesworth SJ (2000) *A phenomenology of working-class experience*. Cambridge: Cambridge University Press.

Cherlin AJ (2014) *Labor's Love Lost: The Rise and Fall of the Working-Class Family in America*. New York: Russell Sage Foundation.

Christin A (2012) Gender and highbrow cultural participation in the United States. *Poetics* 40(5): 423–443.

Coulangeon P and Lemel Y (2007) Is 'distinction' really outdated? Questioning the meaning of the omnivorization of musical taste in contemporary France. *Poetics* 35 (2–3): 93–111.

Council of Europe (2021) *Compendium of Cultural Policies and Trends in Europe.* Available at: www.culturalpolicies.net/ (Accessed 21 August 2022).

Daenekindt S and Roose H (2015) De-institutionalization of high culture? Realized curricula in secondary education in Flanders, 1930–2000. *Cultural Sociology* 9(4): 515–533.

Darrah C (2007) *Busier than ever!: Why American families can't slow down.* Stanford University Press.

De Keere K (2020) Finding the moral space: Rethinking morality, social class and worldviews. *Poetics* 79: 101415.

DiMaggio P (1982) Cultural capital and school success: the impact of status culture participation on the grades of United States high-school students. *American Sociological Review* 47: 189–201.

DiMaggio P and Mukhtar T (2004) Arts participation as cultural capital in the United States, 1982–2002: Signs of decline? *Poetics* 32: 169–194

Du Gay P (1996) *Consumption and identity at work.* London: Sage.

Feder T and Katz-Gerro T (2012) Who benefits from public funding of the performing arts? Comparing the art provision and the hegemony–distinction approaches. *Poetics* 40(4): 359–381.

Gest J (2016). *The new minority. White working class politics in an age of immigration and inequality.* Oxford: Oxford University Press.

Gidron N and Hall P A (2017) The politics of social status: economic and cultural roots of the populist right. *British Journal of Sociology* 68: S57–S84.

Hadley S and Belfiore E (2018) Cultural democracy and cultural policy. *Cultural Trends* 27(3): 218–223.

Harrits GS and Pedersen HH (2019) Symbolic Class Struggles and the Intersection of Socioeconomic, Cultural and Moral Categorisations. *Sociology* 53(5): 861–878.

Heikkilä R and Lindblom T (2022) Overlaps and accumulations: The anatomy of cultural non-participation in Finland, 2007 to 2018. *Journal of Consumer Culture.* Available at: https://doi.org/10.1177/14695405211062052 (Accessed 21 August 2022).

Heilbrun J and Gray C (2001) *The Economics of Art and Culture.* Cambridge: Cambridge University Press.

Hochschild AR (2016) *Strangers in Their Own Land.* New York: The New Press.

Hugrée C, Penissat E and Spire A (2020) *Social Class in Europe. New Inequalities in the Old World.* London: Verso.

Jancovich L (2017) The participation myth. *International Journal of Cultural Policy* 23(1): 107–121.

Jancovich L and Bianchini F (2013) Problematising participation. *Cultural Trends* 22(2): 63–66.

Jancovich L and Ejgod Hansen L (2018) Rethinking participation in the Aarhus as European Capital of Culture 2017 project. *Cultural Trends* 27(3): 173–186.

Jarness V and Flemmen M (2019) A struggle on two fronts: Boundary drawing in the lower region of the social space and the symbolic market for "down-to-earthness". *British Journal of Sociology* 70: 166–189.

Jones O (2016) *Chavs. The demonization of the working class.* London: Verso.

Katz-Gerro T and Jaeger MM (2015) Does Women's Preference for Highbrow Leisure Begin in the Family? Comparing Highbrow Leisure among Brothers and Sisters. *Leisure Sciences* 37(5): 415–430.

Keinan A and Kivetz R (2011) Productivity Orientation and the Consumption of Collectable Experiences. *Journal of Consumer Research* 37(6): 935–950.

McKenzie L (2015) *Getting By. Estates, Class and Culture in Austerity Britain.* London: Policy Press.

Knupfer G (1947) Portrait of the Underdog. *Public Opinion Quarterly* 11(1): 103–114.

Lamont M (2000) *Dignity of Working Men. Morality and the Boundaries of Race, Class, and Immigration.* Cambridge: Harvard University Press.

Lamont M (2018) Addressing Recognition Gaps: Destigmatization and the Reduction of Inequality. *American Sociological Review* 83(3): 419–444.

Lareau A (2011) *Unequal Childhoods. Class, Race, and Family Life.* Berkeley: University of California Press.

Lareau A and Weininger E B (2003) Cultural capital in educational research: A critical assessment. *Theory and Society* 32: 567–606.

Lizardo O (2006) The puzzle of women's "highbrow" culture consumption: Integrating gender and work into Bourdieu's class theory of taste. *Poetics* 34(1): 1–23.

Lizardo O and Skiles S (2012) Reconceptualizing and Theorizing "Omnivorousness": Genetic and Relational Mechanisms. *Sociological Theory* 30(4): 263–282.

López Sintas J and García Álvarez E (2004) Omnivore versus univore consumption and its symbolic properties: evidence from Spaniards' performing arts attendance. *Poetics* 32 (6): 471–491.

Miles A and Sullivan A (2012) Understanding participation in culture and sport: Mixing methods, reordering knowledges. *Cultural Trends* 21(4): 311–324.

Milling J (2019) Valuing cultural participation: The usefulness of the eighteenth-century stage. In: Belfiore E and Gibson L (eds) *Histories of Cultural Participation, Values and Governance.* London: Palgrave Macmillan, pp. 17–41.

Nault JF, Baumann S, Childress C and Rawlings CM (2021) The social positions of taste between and within music genres: From omnivore to snob. *European Journal of Cultural Studies* 24(3): 717–740.

Peterson RA (2005) Problems in comparative research: the example of omnivorousness. *Poetics* 33 (5–6): 257–282.

Peterson RA (1992) Understanding audience segmentation: From elite and mass to omnivore and univore. *Poetics* 21(4): 243–258.

Peterson RA and Kern R (1996) Changing Highbrow Taste: From Snob to Omnivore. *American Sociological Review* 61(5): 900–907.

Peterson RA and Simkus A (1992) How Musical Tastes Mark Occupational Status Groups. In: Lamont M and Fournier M (eds) *Cultivating Differences: Symbolic Boundaries and the Making of Inequality.* Chicago: The University of Chicago Press, pp. 152–186.

Purhonen S, Gronow J and Rahkonen K (2011) Highbrow culture in Finland: Knowledge, taste and participation. *Acta Sociologica* 54(4) 385–402.

Purhonen S, Gronow J, Heikkilä R, Kahma N, Rahkonen K and Toikka A (2014) *Suomalainen maku: Kulttuuripääoma, kulutus ja elämäntyylien sosiaalinen eriytyminen [Finnish taste: Cultural capital, consumption and the social differentiation of lifestyles].* Helsinki: Gaudeamus.

Purhonen S, Heikkilä R, Hazir IK, Lauronen T, Fernández Rodríguez CJ and Gronow J (2019) *Enter culture, exit arts?: The transformation of cultural hierarchies in European newspaper culture sections, 1960–2010.* London: Routlegde.

Roose H and Daenekindt SBL (2015) Trends in cultural participation. In *International Encyclopedia of the Social & Behavioral Sciences* (Second Edition): pp. 447–452.

Salo S and Rydgren J (2021) *The Battle Over Working-Class Voters: How Social Democracy has Responded to the Populist Radical Right in the Nordic Countries.* London: Routledge.

Saukkonen P (2014) *Vankka linnake, joustava sopeutuja vai seisova vesi? Suomalaisen kulttuuripolitiikan viimeaikainen kehitys. [Robust fortress, resilient follower or backwater? The latest developments of Finnish cultural policy.]* Helsinki: Cuporen verkkojulkaisuja 23. Retrieved from http://www.cupore.fi/documents/Kulttuuripolitiikankehitys.pdf

Skarpenes O (2021) Defending the Nordic model: Understanding the moral universe of the Norwegian working class. *European Journal of Cultural and Political Sociology* 8(2): 151–174.

Skeggs B (1997) *Formations of Class and Gender. Becoming respectable.* London: Sage.

Skeggs B and Loveday V (2012) Struggles for Value: Value Practices, Injustice, Judgment, Affect and the Idea of Class. *The British Journal of Sociology* 63(3): 472–490.

Stevenson D (2019) The cultural non-participant: Critical logics and discursive subject identities. *Arts and the Market* 9(1): 50–64.

Stevenson D (2013) What's the problem again? The problematisation of cultural participation in Scottish cultural policy. *Cultural Trends* 22(2): 77–85.

Stevenson D, Balling G and Kann-Rasmussen N (2017) Cultural Participation in Europe: Shared Problem or Shared Problematisation? *International Journal of Cultural Policy* 23(1): 89–106.

Sullivan O and Katz-Gerro T (2007) The Omnivore Thesis Revisited: Voracious Cultural Consumers. *European Sociological Review* 23(2): 123–137.

Tyler I (2013) *Revolting Subjects: Social Abjection and Resistance in Neoliberal Britain.* London: Zed Books.

Veblen T (1889/1953) *The theory of the leisure class.* New York: Macmillan.

Willekens M and Lievens J (2016) Who participates and how much? Explaining non-attendance and the frequency of attending arts and heritage activities. *Poetics* 56: 50–63.

Williams JC (2017) *White Working Class: Overcoming Class Cluelessness in America.* Boston: Harvard Business Review Press.

Willis P (1977/2017) *Learning to Labour: How Working-Class Kids Get Working Class Jobs.* London: Routledge.

Yuksek DA, Dumais SA and Kamo Y (2019) Trends in the relative influence of education and income on highbrow taste, 1982–2012. *Sociological Inquiry* 89(3): 508–531.

CHAPTER 3

What Do We Know About Cultural Participation and Non-participation?

Abstract This chapter deals with the social underpinnings of cultural participation. The most common socio-economic indicators predicting low cultural participation across different national contexts are discussed. It is argued in the light of other empirical studies that the operationalisations are often far from solid and tend to depart from highbrow-oriented participation. This means that many forms of more mundane participation often remain invisible and that activity outside of conventional culture is easily labelled as inactivity or passivity. The everyday participation debate is discussed here as a reminder of the importance of the many informal and locally negotiated cultural practices for understanding cultural participation and non-participation. Finally, it is argued that different understandings of the value of culture are at the heart of the cultural policy debates.

Keywords Cultural participation • Cultural value • Cultural hierarchies • Predictors of cultural non-participation • Everyday participation

© The Author(s) 2022, corrected publication 2023
R. Heikkilä, *Understanding Cultural Non-Participation in an Egalitarian Context*, Palgrave Studies in Cultural Participation,
https://doi.org/10.1007/978-3-031-18865-7_3

THE INTRINSIC LINK BETWEEN SOCIAL POSITION
AND CULTURAL PARTICIPATION

Cultural sociology often departs from the idea that cultural practices are never arbitrary but that they reflect and eventually normalise different kinds of social hierarchies. Cultural participation, in this sense, is a special case and has a social and public dimension, unlike cultural taste or knowledge, because it is visible to others and subject to different public funding policies. Cultural sociology in the tradition of Bourdieu (1984/1979) believes that there is a homological relationship between class and lifestyle, which means that social structures are directly reflected in cultural structures, resulting in shared tastes and cultural participation patterns among different social groups or classes. According to Bourdieu (1984/1979), these patterns are organised hierarchically and create immediate social exclusion, as privileged classes adopt highbrow cultural practices to distinguish themselves from the middle and working classes. The latter, in turn, struggle to navigate the situation the best they can, with the middle classes showing their cultural goodwill by trying to mimic the upper classes, while the popular classes accept their subjugated position by developing popular practices.

Recent research in cultural sociology has proved time and again that, despite the critiques and updates to Bourdieu's theory, which I discussed in the Introduction, his main finding on the link between social and lifestyle hierarchies holds across several national contexts (Chan and Goldthorpe 2007; García-Álvarez et al. 2007; Katz-Gerro and Jaeger 2013; Purhonen et al. 2014). In this book, my main interest lies in the division between cultural participation and non-participation. This division is a direct follow-up to Bourdieu's original idea of the symbolic differences between highbrow and lowbrow cultural practices: researchers have shown beyond doubt that, in various national contexts, active and broad cultural participation is linked to high social status and low cultural participation to low social status (Bennett et al. 2009; Miles and Sullivan 2012; Purhonen et al. 2014; Weingartner and Rössel 2019).

Cultural non-participation and limited cultural participation are extremely common. Most studies have found that more than half of different kinds of societies can be categorised as some type of non-participant. For instance, Weingartner and Rössel (2019), based on their longitudinal survey data from Switzerland, concluded that although the share of their 'inactive' group decreased between 1976 and 2013, it remained sizeable and accounted for approximately one-third of the Swiss population in 2013 (in 1976, the inactive group included almost two thirds of their sample). Reeves and de Vries (2019) reported that 28 per cent of their individual-level panel survey respondents from the UK did not attend any of the 14 activities probed (an additional 23 per cent had attended only one activity). Using their nationally representative Danish sample, Katz-Gerro and Jaeger (2013) showed that 57 per cent of their sample could be categorised as 'passive'. When studying musical tastes in the USA, García-Álvarez et al. (2007) concluded that 56 per cent of their respondents had 'limited' taste. In their study on arts participation in the UK, Chan and Goldthorpe (2007) concluded that as much as 59 per cent of their sample consisted of non-consumers or 'inactives'. In other words, significant portions of various populations can be defined as cultural non-participants. What does this large group look like when scrutinised more closely? My next step will involve looking at the most common socio-economic indicators predicting zero or very low cultural participation across different national contexts.

Education. Generally, all scholarly literature maintains that education is the most important factor structuring and conditioning cultural participation. Cultural activeness is linked to high education, and cultural non-participation is linked to lower education across practically all national contexts (Bennett et al. 2009; Chan and Goldthorpe 2007; García-Álvarez et al. 2007; Katz-Gerro and Jaeger 2013; López-Sintas and García-Álvarez 2002; Purhonen et al. 2014; Reeves and de Vries 2019; Weingartner and Rössel 2019). High educational levels seem to be connected to both the breadth and frequency of cultural participation (Stichele and Laermans 2006). The key role high of education as a structural factor enabling cultural participation is a worthy reminder of the fact that culture and the arts have preserved their position as markers of social status and cultural capital and that Bourdieu's assumption that cultural capital is a skill for navigating the dominant culture and obtaining returns through the formal education system remains directly connected to symbolic domination by the higher classes (Bourdieu and Passeron 1979). However, there are diverging views on how exactly education affects cultural participation. For instance, Reeves and de Vries (2016) showed that although high education generally predicts high cultural participation, the academic disciplines that different individuals have studied have a great effect on participation patterns: humanities degrees are particularly associated with the widest range of cultural participation. Education also seems to have a transgenerational effect: people with the most educated parents end up participating in culture the most (Van Hek and Kraaykamp 2013; Kallunki and Purhonen 2017).

Occupation. Although high education is the single most important factor predicting cultural participation, the impact and direction of occupation is similar but typically somewhat weaker (Purhonen et al. 2011)—for example, executive-level workers exhibit higher levels of cultural participation than the intermediate or working classes. When it comes to specific occupations, Bourdieu himself pointed out that working close to the cultural sectors indicates affinities with highbrow culture (Bourdieu 1984/1979). Subsequent scholars have added that this could partly explain why women tend to participate in highbrow culture more than men (Bihagen and Katz-Gerro 2000). When looking closer at workforce participation and differences in occupational cultures, scholars have argued that arts-related culture in the workplace can serve as a crucial determinant of individual cultural practices (Lizardo 2006). Finally, it should be kept in mind that occupational positions directly function as social networks—for instance, Lauren Rivera's research on elite hiring found that elite evaluators assess not only applicants' CVs and cognitive skills but also, importantly, their leisure interests and cultural participation patterns, which are rewarded for being similar to the evaluators' cultural practices; this finding emphasises the effect and importance of 'cultural matching' (Rivera 2012).

Gender. Practically all studies conclude that men participate in culture less than women, which makes the female gender a strong predictor of active cultural participation and the male gender a predictor of lower participation (Bihagen and Katz-Gerro 2000; Christin 2012; Katz-Gerro 2002; Katz-Gerro and Jæger 2015; Purhonen et al. 2011). No sole explanation has been found for women's higher rates of cultural involvement. Research-based suggestions include arguments that women are more often in charge of the family's cultural status and socialisation (Bihagen and Katz-Gerro 2000), that women experience early socialisation in culture through arts-related hobbies more often than men (Christin 2012) or that women more often work in positions closer to cultural fields than men (Lizardo 2006). Regarding the many different functions that cultural capital can perform in social stratification, scholars have speculated that women play an important role in the 'cultural reproduction model': in the realm of the family, women tend to be responsible for socialisation related to culture (DiMaggio 1982), although there is evidence that the gender difference in highbrow participation could also originate outside of the immediate family context (Katz-Gerro and Jaeger 2015). Finally, the strong impact of gender on cultural participation should always be considered side by side with other contextual indicators—for instance, Lagaert and Roose (2018) have suggested that gender-equal countries have higher numbers of both men and women participating in culture due to greater equality in sharing housework and childcare.

Income. Across most studies, income has been found to have a weaker effect on cultural non-participation than other socio-economic background variables (Chan and Goldthorpe 2007; Heikkilä and Lindblom 2022; Purhonen et al. 2011). Alderson et al. (2007) concluded that the role of income is mostly to *enable* participation: further than that, income does not really distinguish between different modes of cultural participation. Willekens and Lievens (2016) found that economic capital was the only form of capital with zero effect on the propensity to belong to the group of 'non-attenders'. Yaish and Katz-Gerro (2012) made an important contribution by showing that although cultural resources, such as education and inherited cultural capital, affect tastes, income affects actual cultural participation.

Place. Scholars studying the effects of location and access on cultural non-participation often argue that not enough attention is paid to place (see Gilmore 2013; Miles and Gibson 2016). The rationale for emphasising the role of place is that the lack of suitable venues for cultural participation could be a central reason for non-participation and that culturally thriving urban spaces could function as drivers for improving access to culture and enabling the cultural participation of more people. Cutts and Widdop (2017) claimed that people's surroundings are a significant factor structuring participation; according to their study, the extremely active omnivores (whom they call the 'voracious') are associated with big cities with many cultural activities, such as Inner London in the UK. They argued that a suitable context could enhance the possibility of participating in culture—when all other variables were controlled for, one's living area remained an important explanatory factor for cultural participation (Cutts and Widdop 2017). In the same vein, Gayo (2017) found that people living in medium-sized and small cities specifically mentioned the scarcity of possible venues as an obstacle to participating in culture. Gilmore (2017) stressed the important difference between de-commodified and private places—for instance, public parks can become important locations for grassroots cultural participation.

In sum, cultural non-participation is such a complex phenomenon that it cannot be explained but only, at best, *predicted* through certain standard background factors. Other elements to keep in mind include, for instance, digital access, which recent scholarship has found to entail and reproduce exactly the same hierarchies that exist in physical participation (Mihelj et al. 2019), and time constraints. Although lack of time is an often-cited reason for the non-participation of well-off people living busy lives in big cities (Gayo 2017), shift workers, for example, are excluded from traditional event-based cultural participation simply because their timetables do not allow it (Miles and Sullivan 2012). In the family context, it is usually women whose cultural participation suffers due to time constraints (Bihagen and Katz-Gerro 2000); perhaps surprisingly, working full time increases the cultural participation of women but not of men (Willekens and Lievens 2016). Also, context plays an important role for cultural non-participation: the inequality of cultural non-participation varies across countries in relation to wealth and social mobility, with there being less differentiation in highbrow cultural participation in wealthy countries and countries with high social mobility (Van Hek and Kraaykamp 2013).

THE MULTIPLE DEFINITIONS OF CULTURAL PARTICIPATION AND NON-PARTICIPATION

One of the main problems in the scholarly debate on cultural non-participation has been the fact that there are many different yet partly overlapping definitions for it. Terminological differences reflect the variety of the different emphases the phenomenon has been given across time and show that different studies use rather different operationalizations to coin different versions of non-participation.

Most of the operationalisations of cultural non-participation are tightly tied to formal, highbrow-oriented participation. For instance, Chan and Goldthorpe (2007) used the Arts in England survey conducted in 2001 to focus on questions on visual arts that probed whether the participant attended museums and art galleries, exhibitions and collections, craft exhibitions, events including video and electronic art, and cultural festivals; they discovered three types of consumers, among them the 'inactives'. Based on a participation survey conducted in Flanders in 2009 and using the number of visits to arts and heritage events during the last six months, Willekens and Lievens (2016) described the group participating the least as 'non-attendees'. When looking at longitudinal data on US citizens' participation during the last 12 months in the performing, visual and literary arts between 1982 and 2002, López-Sintas and Katz-Gerro (2005) named one of their six different types of patterns of cultural attendance 'passives'.

Recent studies have looked for broader conceptualisations of cultural non-participation and have considered a larger number of variables and indicators beyond traditional highbrow items to measure participation. For instance, based on several waves of the well-known longitudinal and nationally representative British Taking Part survey and taking into account 90 different variables ranging from state-supported highbrow activities to mainstream pastimes such as going to pubs or playing darts, Taylor (2016) concluded that the respondents furthest from active cultural participants can be classified as 'TV viewers'. Miles and Sullivan (2012) combined the Taking Part survey with several qualitative data sets to thoroughly examine the relationship between different forms of participation and non-participation, finding that highbrow non-participation was very common and that, in general, any kind of participation—not only highbrow cultural participation—was linked with health and well-being. Leguina and Miles (2017), once again based on the Taking Part survey, discovered that informal everyday cultural practices functioned as alternatives or possible complements to non-participation. This finding resonates with the consensus of many recent studies, namely, that participating in informal everyday culture at least partly compensates for non-existing participation in traditional formal culture: 'Lack of cultural engagement is compensated for by considerable informal involvement in kin-based and local circles, and in home-based activities' (Bennett et al. 2009, 64).

Everyday Participation

We have seen that conceptualisations of cultural non-participation can be somewhat misleading—they focus on recognised and canonised, legitimate and highbrow-oriented participation, quickly labelling any activity outside of conventional culture as inactivity or passivity. Lately, this myopia has been criticised by several scholars for being derogatory, especially given that the seeming inactivity of low-placed groups in social hierarchies may be a methodological artefact based on an incapacity to capture, or even an unwillingness to see, the informal cultural practices of these groups (cf. Flemmen et al. 2018; Ollivier 2008; Savage et al. 2015). In any case, it seems that starting in the 2010s, studies measuring cultural practices have become more sensitive and more willing to include a wider repertoire of indicators when examining participation. The flourishing debates on 'everyday participation' have played a significant role in this context. The everyday cultural participation approach starts with the notion that 'culture is ordinary' (Williams 1963/1971). Its main ideas stem from the community studies tradition and are based on the central argument that mainstream cultural sociology often disregards the many informal, vernacular, mundane and locally negotiated cultural practices that have little articulated value beyond their immediate contexts (Miles and Gibson

2016). While playing cards, picking mushrooms or being a regular at the local pub might make a person look 'inactive' if measured through mainstream cultural participation surveys emphasising canonised forms of cultural practices, that same person can be said to be extremely active from the perspective of everyday participation—and, in addition, these popular pastimes often overlooked by Bourdieu might have their meticulous social hierarchies and in this sense form entire 'social worlds' (Gronow 2020). Scholars studying everyday participation remind us that a 'careful analysis of the complexities of everyday life can help generate more democratic and more participatory everyday cultural environments' (Ebrey 2016, 158).

One of the main arguments and sociological critiques of the everyday cultural participation debates is the idea presented above: that cultural participation is traditionally defined very narrowly. By adopting a macro approach focusing on the 'seemingly unimportant' aspects in the everyday lives of ordinary people (Back 2015), it is possible to uncover rich cultural participation patterns beyond the narrowly defined and publicly funded highbrow culture. The emphasis on the 'ordinary' or the 'mundane' within the everyday participation tradition links it strongly to working and popular classes (Ebrey 2016). At the same time, there is a strong belief that everyday mundane activities are, in some way, important and cohesive for the 'community' (Gilmore 2017; Miles and Gibson 2016).

The everyday participation debate also calls into question what is valued as culture in society. The different understandings of the value of culture—whether this value is understood as purely cultural and social or simply instrumental and economic—are at the heart of the cultural policy debates (Belfiore 2015). The 'deficit model of cultural participation' (Miles and Gibson 2016) begins with the idea that there is a deficit, or a direct lack, in the participation patterns of the groups with very low cultural participation and that these groups should be nudged towards being more active through different participatory cultural policies. This vicious circle results in implicit hierarchies of cultural participation and ends up mirroring and reproducing these hierarchies in cultural institutions, such as schools and museums. Meanwhile, the people who remain outside these normative participation patterns are seen as isolated and excluded and are further labelled as deviants (Stevenson 2019).

This book intends to expand our idea of cultural participation and to put into practice approaches from the everyday cultural participation debate by trying to understand cultural participation from the perspective of ordinary Finns. At the same time, the book aims to nuance the existing literature by critically assessing the idea that traditional cultural participation and different forms of everyday participation would automatically be complementary counterpoints. It could be that in the Finnish case, everyday participation takes on a less social or community-oriented form than what has been described elsewhere (Bennett et al. 2009; Gilmore 2017).

CONCLUSION: TOWARDS A MORE SENSITIVE WAY OF STUDYING CULTURAL PARTICIPATION

In this chapter, we have seen that cultural participation has strong social underpinnings. Active and broad cultural participation is associated with social privileges, such as high education, and occupations at the middle and top of the hierarchy, which immediately connects non-participation with underprivileged class positions. At the same time, non-participation is extremely common. Therefore, it is surprising how rarely cultural non-participation has been considered a topic of its own.

The terminology and operationalisations of cultural non-participation are far from solid. They tend to depart from a homogeneous understanding of highbrow-oriented cultural practices as the main indicators of whether there is participation at all. The concept of cultural non-participation thus points to a large grey area, given that everything beyond certain preconceived cultural areas is labelled as non-existing participation. One of the aims of this book is to shed light on this grey area using the viewpoints and approaches from the everyday cultural participation debate. The empirical data and methods that have made it possible to undertake this task will be discussed in the next chapter.

REFERENCES

Alderson AS, Junisbai A and Heacock I (2007) Social status and cultural consumption in the United States. *Poetics* 35 (2–3): 191–212.

Back L (2015) Why Everyday Life Matters: Class, Community and Making Life Livable. *Sociology* 49(5): 820–836.

Belfiore E (2015) 'Impact', 'value' and 'bad economics': Making sense of the problem of value in the arts and humanities. *Arts and Humanities in Higher Education* 14(1): 95–110.

Bennett T, Savage M, Silva E, Warde A, Gayo-Cal M and Wright D (2009) *Culture, Class, Distinction*. London: Routledge.

Bihagen E and Katz-Gerro T (2000) Culture consumption in Sweden: The stability of gender differences. Poetics 27 (5–6): 327–349.

Bourdieu P (1984/1979) *Distinction. A Social Critique of the Judgment of Taste.* London: Routledge & Kegan Paul.

Bourdieu P and Passeron JC (1979) *The Inheritors: French Students and Their Relation to Culture.* Chicago, IL: University of Chicago Press.

Chan TW and Goldthorpe JH (2007) Social stratification and cultural consumption: The visual arts in England. *Poetics* 35 (2–3): 168–190.

Christin A (2012) Gender and highbrow cultural participation in the United States. *Poetics* 40(5): 423–443.

Cutts D and Widdop P (2017) Reimagining omnivorousness in the context of place. *Journal of Consumer Culture* 17(3): 480–503.

DiMaggio P (1982) Cultural capital and school success: the impact of status culture participation on the grades of United States high-school students. *American Sociological Review* 47: 189–201.

Ebrey J (2016) The mundane and insignificant, the ordinary and the extraordinary: Understanding Everyday Participation and theories of everyday life. *Cultural Trends* 25(3): 158–168.

Flemmen, M, Jarness, V and Rosenlund, L (2018) Social space and cultural class divisions: The forms of capital and contemporary lifestyle differentiation. *British Journal of Sociology* 69(1): 124–153.

García-Álvarez E, Katz-Gerro T and López-Sintas J (2007) Deconstructing cultural omnivorousness 1982–2002: Heterology in Americans' musical preferences. *Social Forces* 86(2): 417–443.

Gayo M (2017) Exploring Cultural Disengagement: The Example of Chile. *Cultural Sociology* 11(4): 468–488.

Gilmore A (2013) Cold spots, crap towns and cultural deserts: The role of place and geography in cultural participation and creative place-making. *Cultural Trends* 22(2): 86–96.

Gilmore A (2017) The park and the commons: vernacular spaces for everyday participation and cultural value. *Cultural Trends* 26(1): 34–46.

Gronow J (2020) *Deciphering markets and money: a sociological analysis of economic institutions.* Helsinki: Helsinki University Press.

Heikkilä R and Lindblom T (2022) Overlaps and accumulations: The anatomy of cultural non-participation in Finland, 2007 to 2018. *Journal of Consumer Culture.* Available at: https://doi.org/10.1177/14695405211062052 (Accessed 21 August 2022).

Kallunki J and Purhonen S (2017) Intergenerational transmission of cultural capital in Finland. *Research on Finnish Society* 10: 101–111.

Katz-Gerro T (2002) Highbrow Cultural Consumption and Class Distinction in Italy, Israel, West Germany, Sweden, and the United States. *Social Forces* 81(1): 207–229.

Katz-Gerro T and Jaeger MM (2013) Top of the pops, ascend of the omnivores, defeat of the couch potatoes: Cultural consumption profiles in Denmark 1975–2004. *European Sociological Review* 29(2): 243–260.

Katz-Gerro T and Jaeger MM (2015) Does Women's Preference for Highbrow Leisure Begin in the Family? Comparing Highbrow Leisure among Brothers and Sisters. *Leisure Sciences* 37(5): 415–430.

Lagaert S and Roose H (2018) Gender and highbrow cultural participation in Europe: The effect of societal gender equality and development. *International Journal of Comparative Sociology* 59(1): 44–68.

Leguina A and Miles A (2017) Fields of participation and lifestyle in England: revealing the regional dimension from a reanalysis of the Taking Part Survey using Multiple Factor Analysis. *Cultural Trends* 26(1): 4–17.

Lizardo O (2006) The puzzle of women's "highbrow" culture consumption: Integrating gender and work into Bourdieu's class theory of taste. *Poetics* 34(1):1–23.

López-Sintas J and García-Alvarez E (2002) Omnivores show up again: The segmentation of cultural consumers in the Spanish social space. *European Sociological Review* 183(3): 353–368.

López-Sintas J and Katz-Gerro T (2005) From exclusive to inclusive elitists and further: Twenty years of omnivorousness and cultural diversity in arts participation in the USA. *Poetics* 33(5): 299–319.

Mihelj S, Leguina A and Downey J (2019) Culture is digital: Cultural participation, diversity and the digital divide. *New Media & Society* 21(7): 1465–1485.

Miles A and Gibson L (2016) Everyday participation and cultural value. *Cultural Trends* 25(3): 151–157.

Miles A and Sullivan A (2012) Understanding participation in culture and sport: Mixing methods, reordering knowledges. *Cultural Trends* 21(4): 311–324.

Ollivier M (2008) Modes of openness to cultural diversity. Humanist, populist, practical, and indifferent. *Poetics* 36 (2–3): 120–147.

Purhonen S, Gronow J and Rahkonen K (2011) Highbrow culture in Finland: Knowledge, taste and participation. *Acta Sociologica* 54(4): 385–402.

Purhonen S, Gronow J, Heikkilä R, Kahma N, Rahkonen K, Toikka A (2014) *Suomalainen maku: Kulttuuripääoma, kulutus ja elämäntyylien sosiaalinen erityminen [Finnish taste: Cultural capital, consumption and the social differentiation of lifestyles]*. Helsinki: Gaudeamus.

Reeves A and de Vries R (2016) The Social Gradient in Cultural Consumption and the Information-Processing Hypothesis. *The Sociological Review* 64(3): 550–574.

Reeves A and de Vries R (2019) Can cultural consumption increase future earnings? Exploring the economic returns to cultural capital. *British Journal of Sociology* 70: 214–240.

Rivera LA (2012) Hiring as Cultural Matching: The Case of Elite Professional Service Firms. *American Sociological Review* 77(6): 999–1022.

Savage M, Cunningham N, Devine F, Friedman S, Laurison D, McKenzie L, Miles A, Snee H and Wakeling P (2015) *Social Class in the 21st Century*. London: Pelican.

Stevenson D (2019) The cultural non-participant: Critical logics and discursive subject identities. *Arts and the Market* 9(1): 50–64.

Stichele AV and Laermans R (2006) Cultural participation in Flanders: Testing the cultural omnivore thesis with population data. *Poetics* 34: 45–64.

Taylor M (2016) Nonparticipation or Different styles of Participation? Alternative Interpretations from Taking Part. *Cultural Trends* 25(3): 169–181.

Van Hek M and Kraaykamp G (2013) Cultural Consumption across Countries: A Multi-level Analysis of Social Inequality in Highbrow Culture in Europe. *Poetics* 41(4): 323–341

Weingartner S and Rössel J (2019) Changing dimensions of cultural consumption? The space of lifestyles in Switzerland from 1976 to 2013. *Poetics* 74: 101345.

Willekens M and Lievens J (2016) Who participates and how much? Explaining non-attendance and the frequency of attending arts and heritage activities. *Poetics* 56: 50–63.

Williams R (1963/1971) *Culture and society (1780–1950)*. London: Pelican.

Yaish M and Katz-Gerro T (2012) Disentangling 'Cultural Capital': The Consequences of Cultural and Economic Resources for Taste and Participation. *European Sociological Review* 28(2): 169–185.

CHAPTER 4

Defining the Research Object

Abstract This chapter argues that in our era of cultural divides, research-ing cultural practices can be complicated. It is explained that 'lacking' cultural participation appears as something that belongs to the territory of the popular and working classes, which further devalues cultural non-participation. Furthermore, this chapter explains in detail the research design and introduces the data set (40 individual interviews and 9 focus groups) and the sampling strategy. All interviewees could not unambigu-ously be categorised as 'working class', but in general one could character-ise them as 'underprivileged popular classes'. The main analytic tools—close reading and thematic analysis—are explained in detail. It is argued that both individual and focus groups interviews were needed to provide both individual perspectives and common negotiations on the topic.

Keywords Challenges of qualitative interviewing • Close reading • Thematic analysis • Individual interviews • Focus group interviews

ON STUDYING CULTURAL NON-PARTICIPATION AMONG UNDERPRIVILEGED GROUPS

In our era of growing inequalities and increasing politisation and polarisation of lifestyles, researching culture is not an easy task. Daniel DellaPosta used the 'oil spill' metaphor to describe how moral and political divisions have become more accentuated and have started to be increasingly connected to many areas of life that were traditionally not part of political opinions, such as choices of food, clothing or music (DellaPosta 2020). When starting to collect empirical data for this book, I sensed that cultural participation, however defined, could be a touchy topic to study empirically, especially among people whose cultural practices could be situated rather far from traditional or normative ones. Qualitative interviews always create and reinforce power dynamics (Bengtsson and Fynbo 2018; MacLure et al. 2010). Therefore, I expected that this subject matter would be especially prone to teasing them out because culture and cultural participation could appear as elitist topics of conversation, thus further emphasising pre-existing hierarchies between the researcher and the interviewees.

One of the main motivations for this book was that cultural non-participation is often characterised as a mere 'lack' of cultural participation, as a privation of something that ideally should exist. Cultural non-participation is, even linguistically speaking, the opposite of 'engagement' or 'participation'. In the existing scholarly research, the role attributed to cultural non-participation has usually been that of a necessary counterpoint to middle-class cultural practices. This has automatically made 'lacking' cultural participation appear as something that belongs firmly to the territory of the popular and working classes, which, as has been discussed, devalues cultural non-participation and assigns it a certain stigma (Bennett et al. 2009; Charlesworth 2000; Devine et al. 2005). Bourdieu himself has been claimed to neglect the richness of the culture of the working classes because he saw them as passive and willing to accept, as he coined it, the 'taste of necessity'. According to this idea, economic scarcity makes working classes unable to develop specific tastes, which is why they supposedly create tastes and entire lifestyles around modesty, functionality and practicality (Bourdieu 1984/1979, 378–379; see also Blasius and Friedrichs 2008).

Among others, Tony Bennett (2011) pointed out severe shortcomings in Bourdieu's approach regarding the working and popular classes.

According to Bennett, Bourdieu refuses to see the working classes as possessors of their own aesthetic and cultural tastes, thus depriving them 'of any possible positive content except for purely defensive practices' (Bennett 2011, 523). Regarding methodology, Bennett argued that Bourdieu's working classes were underrepresented in the latter's sample for the empirical analysis of *Distinction*; they were not treated with the same methodological rigour as the middle and upper classes, and hence the questions posed were biased, providing the working classes with very limited possibilities of exhibiting the cultural practices and forms of capitals relevant in their lives (Bennett 2011). According to Bennett's formulation (2011, 531), Bourdieu's account of working-class culture is informed by 'absolute aesthetic, cultural, and political closure'.

This idea of cultural disengagement as first and foremost a 'lack' or a form of closure is reflected in the fact that cultural participation is, in virtually all scholarly research, associated with privileged positions in society. High education predicts active cultural participation, whereas cultural non-participation is linked to lower education (Bennett et al. 2009; Chan and Goldthorpe 2007; García-Álvarez et al. 2007; Katz-Gerro and Jaeger 2013; López-Sintas and García-Álvarez 2002; Purhonen et al. 2014; Reeves and de Vries 2019). The same goes for high occupational class (Purhonen et al. 2011). Active cultural participation even predicts better future income, including when other factors are accounted for (Reeves and de Vries 2019). Empirical studies directly link active cultural participation with happiness and life satisfaction (Ateca-Amestoy 2011; Wheatley and Bickerton 2017). Active cultural participation even seems to be connected to good physical health: empirical studies have convincingly shown that the more active people are culturally, the better their health is, even when other socio-economic variables are taken into consideration (Hyyppä et al. 2006; Konlaan et al. 2000).

All of this, of course, reflects the fact that most existing research on cultural practices is completely biased in favour of middle-class practices, both in terms of topics and methods (Bennett 2011; Bunting et al. 2019; Flemmen et al. 2018; Miles 2016). When surveys on cultural practices typically involve items such as reading books, attending the theatre and listening to classical music, it is no wonder that many people from working and popular classes end up looking passive or disengaged. In the same vein, prioritising quantitative methods over qualitative methods and reducing entire cultural fields to easily comparable indicators strengthens canonical ways of measuring cultural participation (cf. Bunting et al.

2019). In short, traditional nationally representative surveys are a poor reflection of the activities and pastimes that fall outside the middle-class canon. In this context, Flemmen et al. (2018, 23) remind scholars of cultural stratification that they 'should be much more careful in their description of the tastes of the lower class, especially in applying morally derogative terms to significant sections of the population on the basis of what might very well be inadequacies in research methods or data'. It can thus be claimed that macro-scale research instruments measuring conventional cultural practices are, at least to some extent, simply incapable of properly grasping and understanding the leisure time of less privileged classes.

A related challenge of studying culturally disengaged groups—which can be turned into a motivation on why they *should* be studied—is that they are usually underrepresented answering different surveys and even consenting to different kinds qualitative studies (Purhonen et al. 2014, 423; Savage et al. 2015). I solved this particular problem by using previous quantitative research to determine which factors predict low cultural participation and then zooming in more closely on particular groups through qualitative interviews. Despite their limitations, qualitative interviews are one of the best ways of mapping embodied perceptions, opinions, values and attitudes (Kvale and Brinkmann 2009). Interviews on cultural practices with people with possibly little interest or experience in culture might be particularly full of discourses of potentialities and possibilities: for instance, Lamont and Swidler (2014) underlined the unique capacity of interviews in helping us to understand the underlying or latent life-worlds of the interviewees.

PROBLEMS AND CHALLENGES IN INTERVIEWS

Conducting qualitative interviews usually means confronting many kinds of challenges and problems, some of them predictable and others surprising. Again, interviews on culture with participants who potentially have very little interest and investment in culture can be expected to be particularly challenging. Typical problems discussed in the rich methodological literature on qualitative interviewing include, first, interviewees' reluctance to be interviewed, which typically manifests itself in difficulties finding interviewees or encountering different types of resistance during the interview (Heikkilä and Katainen 2021). Second, sometimes researchers can encounter silence: in focus groups, silence can mean that group members have difficulties sharing their 'real' thoughts with the rest of the group (Hollander 2004). On the other hand, silence offers both interviewers and interviewees tools to operate in the interview situation—for example, for an interviewee, silence can function as a means of not being labelled as 'socially deviant' (Bengtsson and Fynbo 2018). Third, even if interviewees are willing to talk, they may refuse to provide the specific information that the researcher is looking for (Lareau 1996, 2011) by being ironic and exaggerating (Savage et al. 2015), or they may lack suitable skills to navigate the formal interview situation (Silva and Wright 2005). Finally, whether dealing with individual interviews or focus groups, dominating interviewees can create conversational challenges—for instance, in a group situation, an extremely dominating interviewee may express normative hegemonic views that make it difficult for other interviewees to get their voices heard (Smithson 2000).

Many researchers argue that these challenges related to interview situations should be considered part of what qualitative research actually is: the different problems and challenges foreground the many power relations at play and highlight agendas that the researcher may not have initially thought of (Jacobsson and Åkerström 2012; Katainen and Heikkilä 2020; Vitus 2008). There is wide scholarly support for the idea that researchers should give particular analytical space to the 'failed' and 'negative' parts of interviews (or entire interviews) because different kinds of challenges may help better discern the power dynamics of the interview, thus improving one's understanding of the meaning-making processes of the situation (Bengtsson and Fynbo 2018; Jacobsson and Åkerström 2012; MacLure et al. 2010).

As discussed above, one can expect such challenges to be amplified when studying the cultural practices of people who are expected to engage in few cultural practices or to participate in practices that are very far from more conventional cultural participation. I have already treated elsewhere the many problematic aspects of the interviews that form the empirical basis of this book (Heikkilä and Katainen 2021). When closely analysing the 'counter-talk' that emerged in the interviews, understood as implicit or explicit disruptions of the conversation, it was noticed that the counter-talk was typically directed either towards the interview situation, the topic or the interviewer. The main conclusion drawn in the article was that the problems and challenges inherent in different qualitative interview situations should be given more emphasis in analyses and that 'counter-talk' can also be examined as moral boundary-drawing (cf. Lamont 1992); in fact, topics related to culture are especially fruitful for encountering such boundaries. The different types of counter-talk will be explored more closely in the empirical part of this book.

RESEARCH DESIGN AND DATA

The idea behind the data collection process for this study was to produce a theoretical sample of interviewees whose background profiles would match statistical factors predicting low cultural participation. The theoretical sampling was done by means of two pre-existing nationally representative Finnish surveys, *Culture and Leisure in Finland 2007* ($N = 1388$) and *Finnish Views on and Engagement in Culture and the Arts 2013* ($N = 7859$), on cultural taste and participation. To find out which background factors predicted zero or low cultural participation, I used two survey questions on visiting places related to culture and the arts, including both highbrow and lowbrow items. Statistically significant factors for low cultural participation were low education, living far from large cities, living in northern or eastern Finland, having a manual occupation and having a position outside the traditional labour market—for example, being on pension, a farmer, unemployed or on parental leave. The interview sample was formed with the idea that each interviewee should exhibit at least four of these statistically significant indicators of low cultural participation. Education was considered such an important factor in structuring and conditioning cultural participation (Bennett et al. 2009; Bourdieu 1984/1979; Purhonen et al. 2014) that none of the interviewees had a university degree (see the Appendices for a more detailed description).

Why use both individual interviews and focus groups? The underlying idea was to gain access to the advantages offered by both types of data. I expected that focus groups would be useful in travelling beyond individual perspectives by providing access to the discourses that people had on the studied topic and showing how they negotiated it in formal settings (Harrits and Pedersen 2019; Heikkilä and Katainen 2021; Silva and Wright 2005). At the same time, I expected that individual interviews would add depth to the discourses discovered through the focus groups and provide the informants with a sense of intimacy that focus groups usually lack (Silverman 2014). The focus groups were so-called naturally occurring groups—participants who already knew one another (Heikkilä 2008; Wilkinson 1998). To facilitate recruitment, potential focus groups were contacted via institutional actors, such as vocational schools, associations and the national church of Finland (the Evangelical Lutheran Church of Finland, the largest religious body in the country). Interviewed groups included vocational school students studying fields related to machinery and nursing, individuals from different pensioners' associations in small towns, unemployed persons from several employment rehabilitation centres, regulars of a local bar of a small city and a group receiving free meals organised by the church.

The recruitment of individual interviewees was a particularly challenging task, and I had to use many different techniques to arrive at a sufficiently rich sample. First, existing contacts helped find potential participants with suitable profiles, both individuals and groups. Then, snowballing was used—for instance, many interviewed women managed to persuade their husbands to participate in the interviews after they themselves had been interviewed. Finally, different local groups, such as pensioners' or unemployed workers' associations and vocational education institutions, were used to recruit interviewees. As a last step, and after carefully analysing what kinds of profiles were still missing from the sample—typically young, urban men, either unemployed or working in manual jobs—a research agency was contacted to recruit suitable profiles. The interviewees recruited through the research agency were offered a gift card of a local supermarket chain—a policy recommended by the agency to ensure the interviewees would turn up. All interviews were organised and held by me in public places chosen to best suit the interviewees—in the case of the individual interviews, these were typically cafés, free meeting rooms in public libraries and, in some cases (especially in the countryside), interviewees' homes. The focus group interviews were organised in whatever place the group would meet at regularly: these were churches, different associations' meeting spaces, vocational schools' classrooms and again, in some cases, interviewees' homes. The individual interviews lasted for approximately 45 minutes each, while the focus groups lasted for approximately 1 hour. Altogether 40 individual interviews and 9 focus groups collected in spring 2018 all over Finland form the data used in this book.

The topic guide for the interviews followed the models of several recent studies on cultural practices, most importantly of the sub-study from the British National Child Development Study (Elliott et al. 2010) and of the Finnish Cultural Capital and Social Differentiation in Contemporary Finland research project (Purhonen et al. 2014). The interviews were targeted to be loosely defined 'participation narratives'—interviewees' life stories without the intention of portraying participation as necessarily cultural (see Miles 2016). All interviews included open-ended and closed-ended questions and touched on both overarching topics, such as leisure in general, and cultural participation and non-participation more closely; all interviews included an art-photo-elicitation part. Detailed interview guidelines and a list of the photographs used are provided in the Appendices.

Given that all interviewees had low education and that most had or had previously held manual occupations often running across generations, as can be seen in the interviewees' background profiles presented in the Appendices, it was tempting to categorise them simply as 'working class'. However, this category is far from watertight on many occasions. Some interviewees were students, some had never worked, some were long-term unemployed, some were 'between jobs', and some were outside of the labour market because they were on parental leave or on pension for various reasons. Elsewhere, I categorised my interviewees as 'underprivileged popular classes' (see Heikkilä 2021), which I think is a more adequate and flexible characterisation for the many kinds of life situations in which the interviewees found themselves. Obviously, some of my interviewees were much more underprivileged than others—many were unemployed, some were on disability pension, some were going through processes of debt adjustment, or some were looking for housing, while others were working or studying in more stable and secure economic and social conditions.

The Finnish case, introduced in more detail in the Introduction, was thoroughly reflected in the sample. Finland has a small number of immigrants compared to most other European countries—for instance, the percentage of persons with a foreign background for the years 2018, 2019 and 2020 was 7.3 per cent, 7.7 per cent and 8.0 per cent, respectively (Official Statistics of Finland 2021). The largest integrated language minority were the Finnish Swedes, one of the few minorities in the world that do better according to most socio-economic indicators than the language majority, but they only account for approximately 5 per cent of the Finnish population (Heikkilä 2011; Official Statistics of Finland 2021). Therefore, the sample was, except for one immigrant in one of the focus groups, deliberately composed of only Finnish-speaking ethnic Finns.

In this book, the main analytic tool was a rigorous close reading of all the interviews, followed by thematic analysis (Silverman 2014). Originally, the main aim of the close reading was to identify the different modes of cultural engagement (cf. Heikkilä 2015), which I categorised elsewhere as social-mundane, cultural-legitimate and introvert-hostile (Heikkilä 2021).

As the analysis proceeded, I understood that the different modes of cultural engagement were not the whole story; a much deeper division lay behind the interviewees' approaches, attitudes and discourses on the enormous normative demand to participate in culture, which has been thoroughly discussed in the previous chapters. This made the analysis first run through the following questions: What do the interviewees' life-worlds look like? What kinds of things do their daily lives consist of—where, when and with whom? Are there orientations towards highbrow or popular culture, towards forms of 'everyday participation' or towards something entirely different? Then, I proceeded to the following questions: How do the interviewees understand and describe their own participation? What kinds of symbolic boundaries are drawn in the interviews? What attitudes do the interviewees have towards others' perceived participation? Are there signs of cultural goodwill, hostility, tolerance or something else? Finally, I attempted to systematically scrutinise the attitudes towards cultural participation by asking the following questions: How is normative cultural participation discussed in the interviews? How do the interviewees frame themselves as participants, if at all?

It should be stressed that I was not looking to cluster the interviewed individuals and groups into specific categories but to identify larger discourses that individual interviewees would mobilise. In this book, the analysis—and also the three empirical Chaps. 5, 6 and 7—will present three overarching themes based on the attitudes that the interviewees had towards cultural participation: 'affirmation', 'functionality' and 'resistance'.

Regarding ethical issues, all interviewees were informed openly and comprehensively, both during recruitment (in writing) and again before the interview (orally), of the following topics: the researcher's contact information along with detailed information about the funding of the study, the topic and objectives of the research, the means of collecting the data, the voluntary nature of participation, the provision of full confidentiality and the fact that the data would be transcribed and anonymised for publications and archived for possible further research use. Given that the data were collected directly from the informants without combining personal information to, for instance, register the data, the data were anonymised, and the topic was not considered sensitive according to the Finnish Personal Data Act (523/1999); oral consent for the interviews was considered sufficient. The data were transcribed by a professional transcriber and anonymised by the author, carefully following the guidelines of the Finnish Social Science Data Archive. The entire data, together with relevant metadata, such as the exact dates of the interviews, has been delivered to the Finnish Social Science Data Archive for possible future research use.

CONCLUSION: WHY INTERVIEWS?

The aim of this chapter has been to provide a detailed account of the empirical data consisting of a theoretical sample of people with background factors predicting low cultural participation and to discuss why the particular interview selection process was potentially the most suitable data gathering method for the study.

In tracing what cultural non-participation means in cultural stratification research, this chapter has argued that cultural non-participation is typically presented as the negative counterpoint of active cultural participation strongly associated with the middle classes and depicted as a 'lack' of something that should be in place. This bias, partly inherited from Bourdieu (1984/1979), easily neglects and overlooks the potentially rich and active lifestyles led by people and groups beyond the traditional scope of cultural participation. It only makes the situation more complicated that the act of filling out surveys measuring conventional cultural participation seems to be closely related to cultural participation itself—people with little traditional cultural participation are underrepresented in answering surveys and also in participating in different kinds of qualitative interviews.

It is for this reason that I argue that studying potential cultural non-participants through qualitative techniques, namely, interviews, is a good idea: interviews can be helpful in teasing out different embodied perceptions, values and motivations that are difficult to access through other qualitative techniques, such as ethnographic observation or accounts produced independently by the people studied. The following empirical part of the book will put to the test how well the individual and focus group interviews captured the interviewees' everyday lives and participation.

REFERENCES

Ateca-Amestoy V (2011) Leisure and subjective well-being. In: Cameron S (ed) *Handbook on the Economics of Leisure*. Cheltenham: Edward Elgar.
Charlesworth SJ (2000) *A phenomenology of working-class experience*. Cambridge: Cambridge University Press.

DellaPosta D (2020) Pluralistic Collapse: The "Oil Spill" Model of Mass Opinion Polarization. *American Sociological Review* 85(3): 507–536.

Bengtsson TT and Fynbo L (2018) Analysing the significance of silence in qualitative interviewing: Questioning and shifting power relations. *Qualitative Research* 18(1): 19–35.

Bennett T (2011) Culture, choice, necessity: A political critique of Bourdieu's aesthetic. *Poetics* 39: 530–546.

Bennett T, Savage M, Silva E, Warde A, Gayo-Cal M and Wright D (2009) *Culture, Class, Distinction*. London: Routledge.

Blasius J and Friedrichs J (2008) Lifestyles in distressed neighborhoods: A test of Bourdieu's "taste of necessity" hypothesis. *Poetics* 36(1): 24–44.

Bourdieu P (1984/1979) *Distinction. A Social Critique of the Judgment of Taste*. London: Routledge & Kegan Paul.

Bunting C, Gilmore A and Miles A (2019) Calling participation to account: Taking part in the politics of method. In Belfiore E and Gibson L (eds) *Histories of Cultural Participation, Values and Governance*. London: Palgrave, pp. 183–210.

Chan TW and Goldthorpe JH (2007) Social stratification and cultural consumption: The visual arts in England. *Poetics* 35(2–3): 168–190.

Devine F, Savage M, Scott J and Crompton R (2005) (eds) *Rethinking Class: Culture, Identities and Lifestyles*. London: Palgrave Macmillan.

Elliott J, Miles A, Parsons S and Savage M (2010) The design and content of the 'Social Participation' study: A qualitative sub-study conducted as part of the age 50 (2008) sweep of the National Child Development Study. Centre for Longitudinal Studies.

Flemmen, M, Jarness, V and Rosenlund, L (2018) Social space and cultural class divisions: The forms of capital and contemporary lifestyle differentiation. *British Journal of Sociology* 69(1): 124–153.

García-Álvarez E, Katz-Gerro T and López-Sintas J (2007) Deconstructing cultural omnivorousness 1982–2002: Heterology in Americans' musical preferences. *Social Forces* 86(2): 417–443.

Harrits GS and Pedersen HH (2019) Symbolic Class Struggles and the Intersection of Socioeconomic, Cultural and Moral Categorisations. *Sociology* 53(5): 861–878.

Heikkilä R (2008) Puhuva ryhmä. Ryhmähaastattelun käytöstä sosiaalitieteellisessä tutkimusasetelmassa. [The speaking group. On using focus groups in social research.] *Sosiologia* 45(4): 292–305.

Heikkilä, Riie (2015). Suomalainen maku ja kulttuurin kuluttamisen valikoituneisuus. [Finnish taste and exclusive cultural consumption.] In Arto Lindholm (ed.) *Ei-kävijästä osalliseksi. Osallistuminen, osallistaminen ja osallisuus kulttuurialalla*. Helsinki: Humak. 33–52.

Heikkilä R (2011) *Bättre folk, bättre smak? Suomenruotsalaisten maku ja kulttu-uripääoma.* [*Better people, better taste? Taste and cultural capital among the Finnish Swedes.*] Helsingin yliopisto: Sosiaalitieteiden laitoksen julkaisuja 2011: 5. Available at: http://urn.fi/URN:ISBN:978-952-10-6693-1 (Accessed 21 August 2022).

Heikkilä R (2021) The slippery slope of cultural non-participation: Orientations of participation among the potentially passive. *European Journal of Cultural Studies* 24: 202–219.

Heikkilä R and Katainen A (2021) Counter-talk as symbolic boundary drawing: Challenging legitimate cultural practices in individual and focus group interviews in the lower regions of social space. *Sociological Review* 69: 1029–1050.

Hollander JA (2004) The Social Context of Focus Groups. *Journal of Contemporary Ethnography* 33(5): 602–637.

Jacobsson K and Åkerström M (2012) Interviewees with an agenda: Learning from a 'failed' interview. *Qualitative Research* 13(6): 717–734.

Hyyppä M, Mäki J, Impivaara O and Aromaa A (2006). Leisure participation predicts survival: A population-based study in Finland. *Health Promotion International* 21: 5–12.

Katainen A and Heikkilä R (2020) Analysing the ways of participating in interview settings: Young people's identity performances and social class in focus groups. *Qualitative Research* 20(5): 649–666.

Katz-Gerro T and Jaeger MM (2013) Top of the pops, ascend of the omnivores, defeat of the couch potatoes: Cultural consumption profiles in Denmark 1975–2004. *European Sociological Review* 29(2): 243–260.

Konlaan BB, Bygren LO and Johansson SE (2000) Visiting the cinema, concerts, museums or art exhibitions as determinant of survival: a Swedish fourteen-year cohort follow-up. *Scandinavian Journal of Public Health* 28: 174–178.

Kvale S and Brinkmann S (2009) *Inter Views. Learning the craft of qualitative research interviews.* London: Sage.

Lamont M (1992) *Money, Morals and Manners: The Culture of the French and American Upper Middle Classes.* Chicago: University of Chicago Press.

Lamont M and Swidler A (2014) Methodological pluralism and the possibilities and limits of interviewing. *Qualitative Sociology* 37(2): 153–171

Lareau A (1996) Common problems in fieldwork: A personal essay. In Lareau A and Shultz J (eds) *Journeys through ethnography: Realistic accounts of* fieldwork. Boulder, CA: Westview Press, pp. 195–236.

Lareau A (2011) *Unequal Childhoods. Class, Race, and Family Life.* Berkeley: University of California Press.

López-Sintas J and García-Alvarez E (2002) Omnivores show up again: The segmentation of cultural consumers in the Spanish social space. *European Sociological Review* 183(3): 353–368.

MacLure M, Holmes R, Jones L and MacRae C (2010) Silence as resistance to analysis: Or, on not opening one's mouth properly. *Qualitative Inquiry* 16(6): 492–500.

Miles A (2016) Telling tales of participation: exploring the interplay of time and territory in cultural boundary work using participation narratives. *Cultural Trends* 25(3): 182–193.

Official Statistics of Finland (2021) Population structure [online publication]. ISSN=1797-5395. Helsinki: Statistics Finland. Available at: https://stat.fi/en/publication/cl8k6idagdoy60cw1ctrrw058 (Accessed 31 October 2022)

Personal Data Act 523/1999. Available at: http://www.finlex.fi/en/laki/kaannokset/1999/19990523 (Accessed 21 August 2022).

Purhonen S, Gronow J, Heikkilä R, Kahma N, Rahkonen K, Toikka A (2014) *Suomalainen maku: Kulttuuripääoma, kulutus ja elämäntyylien sosiaalinen eriytyminen [Finnish taste: Cultural capital, consumption and the social differentiation of lifestyles]*. Helsinki: Gaudeamus.

Purhonen S, Gronow J and Rahkonen K (2011) Highbrow culture in Finland: Knowledge, taste and participation. *Acta Sociologica* 54(4): 385–402.

Reeves A and de Vries R (2019) Can cultural consumption increase future earnings? Exploring the economic returns to cultural capital. *British Journal of Sociology* 70: 214–240.

Savage M, Cunningham N, Devine F, Friedman S, Laurison D, McKenzie L, Miles A, Snee H and Wakeling P (2015) *Social Class in the 21st Century*. London: Pelican.

Silva EB and Wright D (2005) The judgement of taste and social position in focus group research. *Sociologia e Ricerca Sociale* 76–77: 241–253.

Silverman D (2014) *Interpreting qualitative data*. London: Sage.

Smithson J (2000) Using and analysing focus groups: Limitations and possibilities. *International Journal of Social Research Methodology* 3(2): 103–119.

Vitus K (2008) The agonistic approach: Reframing resistance in qualitative research. *Qualitative Inquiry* 14(3): 466–488.

Wheatley D and Bickerton C (2017) Subjective well-being and engagement in arts, culture and sport. *Journal of Cultural Economics* 41: 23–45.

Wilkinson S (1998) Focus group methodology: a review. *International Journal of Social Research Methodology* 3(1), 181–203.

PART II

Cultural Milieus of the "Potentially Passive"

CHAPTER 5

Affirmation

Abstract This chapter focuses on the first out of three discourses found in the data. This 'affirmation discourse' emphasises the importance of both traditional highbrow-oriented participation and different kinds of everyday participation. In the affirmation discourse, the idea that participating in culture is 'good for you' is taken seriously. Culture is attributed an unquestionable intrinsic value. It can be interpreted that the affirmation discourse still has confidence in the power of cultural participation to function as a mechanism for providing cultural capital. In the affirmation discourse, the only boundaries are drawn downwards, and there seems to be an inherent idea of adjusting to the hegemonic discourse whereby one must participate in culture. It is argued that the affirmation discourse characterises the egalitarian worldviews of high conformity.

Keywords Affirmation discourse • Cultural goodwill • Cultural capital • Egalitarianism • Downward symbolic boundaries

PROLOGUE

When she comes to meet me on the porch of her snow-surrounded house, Alma, a 69-year-old woman who lives on a family farm in a small countryside village in the north of Finland, hugs me warmly as if we were old

© The Author(s) 2022, corrected publication 2023
R. Heikkilä, *Understanding Cultural Non-Participation in an Egalitarian Context*, Palgrave Studies in Cultural Participation,
https://doi.org/10.1007/978-3-031-18865-7_5

friends. She receives me in her traditional countryside farmhouse filled
with paintings by local artists and relatives and immediately starts serving
me coffee and homemade buns.

As a child, as her father was the local station master, Alma lived by the
railroad ('When I heard the sound of the train, it was like being at home').
After finishing basic education, she worked for a while in an office but
soon met her future husband, a farmer. Since then, Alma worked her
whole life as a farmer's wife with plenty of family members living in the
vicinity and has never complained or shunned hard work ('It was rough,
we had a hundred animals and thirty cows, and it was just the two of us –
I've also driven the tractor when needed'). After retiring some years ago,
Alma made up her mind to remain active ('I decided that this grandma
won't stay lying in bed') and frequently mentions that she simply cannot
stay still ('I cannot just sleep, not even on holidays'). This means that she
works around the house and maintains the grounds, bakes bread for selling it in the local marketplace and mows the lawn; in addition, she has
joined a volleyball team and a water aerobics group, both of which meet
twice a week. Alma is extremely social—even though she lives in a small
village, she sees other people regularly in different events and prides herself on her sociable attitude ('I always meet acquaintances even if I don't
know them yet ... I'm a person that might just start to talk'). Her phone
keeps ringing even as I interview her. Alma also volunteers for a church
social work group that brings old people together for talks and activities.
She has two children who used to be active in sports associations in their
youth and that now live in the capital area of Finland. She has stayed in
close touch with them and her large group of grandchildren.

Alma has been very busy travelling, especially in the Nordic countries
and in Finland. Her trips are mostly for relaxation and socialisation ('I
always go for treatments – massage, haircut, pedicure, manicure, everything – that has been so relaxing, and then of course, during different
celebrations, one has to go around Finland seeing relatives'). Alma reads a
lot, especially historical novels, and recently, she has gotten into audio-
books. She has only occasionally been to concerts of classical music and
never to the opera, but she basically attends any event that is brought to
the cultural centres of the closest larger towns and cities ('We used to
always book a bus and go there together with a larger group'). These
events mostly include different classical music concerts and plays. Alma
draws basically no symbolic boundaries towards anything or anyone except
for gossip magazines which she is critical of ('I don't like Seiska, I have

sometimes browsed it at the hairdresser's') and some Finnish male writers ('…maybe it's because he so often talks about the private parts, but well, it does not really bother me, I know how to leap over those bits'). Usually, she likes more or less everything that is introduced into her universe.

MORE ACTIVE THAN THE MIDDLE CLASSES?

The above presented Alma is a good example of the main elements of the 'affirmation' discourse. First, this discourse endorses completely normative cultural participation. Alma happily participates in whatever is brought to her at the local cultural centre and feels completely at home attending concerts of classical music or theatre performances. Second, the affirmation discourse embraces the ideal of being active and busy and maintaining lifelong activity. Alma has consciously shunned a lazy life, occupying herself with the realms of both culture, sports, popular culture and social life, with a strong emphasis on not staying at home.

We know from previous research that cultural activity and engagement in itself are distinctive (Heikkilä and Lindblom 2022; Prieur and Savage 2013; Purhonen et al. 2014; Weingartner and Rössel 2019): the fundamental division seems to run between the people who participate abundantly in culture and those who mostly abstain from it. Moreover, we know that being busy is also a sign of status distinction. As the Finnish writer Juha Itkonen has aptly put it, 'The entire middle class runs away from death in their expensive gear, they run to stay on the fast track, they run to repel the anxiety that is after them' (Itkonen 2009). Sociologist Hartmut Rosa speaks of a 'social acceleration' (Rosa 2013), whereby everyday life is conducted at an increasingly high pace due to the accelerated nature of technology and social changes, which introduces a fundamental aspect of busyness into our lives. What is important here is that this feeling of the 'shrinking of the present' (Rosa 2013) does not necessarily affect everyone in the same way; rather, it is an essentially socially structured perception. For instance, Oriel Sullivan notes that it is the 'income rich and time poor' individuals that mainly use busyness as a means of status distinction (Sullivan 2008).

This idea of busyness and activity as an ideal is strongly recognisable in the affirmation discourse. Many interviewees come from strong working-class backgrounds, and the idea of being constantly on the move is an important building block for their identities. There is 'no need to twiddle one's thumbs', like Henrik, a 68-year-old pensioner bus driver puts it.

Tuomo, a 77-year-old pensioner who comes from a farmer background like both Henrik and the above-described Alma, sums it up by referring to another study:

> Some years ago they did a survey (...) about what was the most dangerous piece of furniture of the house, it said that a kitchen stool is something that you can easily fall from, but I personally think the living room sofa is more dangerous. If you start lazying on the sofa, that's a problem.

The probably busiest person of the whole data is Julia, a 68-year hairdresser on pension. She seems to value activeness over everything else and has a tight regular schedule for each day of the week, including weekends:

> Mondays I first have yoga at 11 o'clock, then I have my daily walk, I have to walk one hour at least four times a week. And then Tuesday is a day that I can decide myself what I do, and many times it becomes a day for skiing or something like that, also depending on the weather. If I'm tired I don't go anywhere, but that rarely happens, and then on Wednesdays I have this gymnastics class and then in the daytime I go to this polka dance or Finnish folk dance hobby. Then on Thursday I go to the gym and then swimming, to the swimming hall I go walking. I walk for half an hour and then I do aqua jogging for half of an hour. On Friday I have stage dancing. (...) On Saturday I have a free day that I also most often use for dancing or partying somewhere. (...) On Sunday I have also yoga, another yoga in which I am in the executive committee of the association.

A younger and highly similar example is 37-year-old Sami, who is a cook at a restaurant. He talks abundantly about the fact that although his work shifts are physically very straining and that he is separated from his partner and sometimes spends time with his child, he still has the energy to do many things on his free time. For instance, he plays disc golf ('the shorter route is a good six kilometers, and you are carrying a backpack of 20 kilograms in a mixed terrain'), makes his own cosmetic products from the beeswax that he buys online, volunteers as an administrator of a computer game, brews his own beers and is the president of his housing cooperative. The last activity typically requires especially administrative work, but Sami has also volunteered to participate in the pipeline renovation of the house, which is typically an enormous, skill-dependent operation. When asked how he manages to do everything, he downplays his own role, saying, 'Well, I like to take on these kinds of projects'.

The ideal of activity is present even in individual profiles that otherwise are quite critical of cultural participation as such (and who we will meet in Chap. 7). For instance, Marko, a 47-year-old farmer with no formal education and with a largely hostile attitude towards traditional highbrow culture states:

> RH: Do you have any moments when you are not doing anything? Kind of just lying on the sofa or…?
> Marko: Well, I just don't feel at home simply lying around. If I lay down on the sofa, I need something like a sudoku or a crossword.

Meanwhile, within the affirmation discourse there is plenty of evidence of also traditional cultural participation which is often discussed in highly passionate tones. This is the case of Eeva, a 65-year-old retired nurse who describes her relationship with reading as an obsession that prevents her from doing anything else before a certain book is finished:

> Reading has always been for me kind of a passion. (…) Since I was young I've liked reading and have read a lot. Probably it was the mother tongue teacher at school, at middle school, who kind of opened these doors of literature. But I remember, from the times when the children were small, that I sometimes received some book for Mother's Day, and that I read that book during Mother's Day and over the evening, it might have been two o'clock in the morning, and I would still be lying on my back on the sofa and reading the book, I just had to finish it. (…) I still have this thing that if I go to the library and borrow books, if there is a book that… like I said, that just really captivates me, I can't do anything before I have finished that book, even if I'm not able anymore to read it non-stop. But well, then I rest my eyes for a moment and then I read again. When I have a book at hand, all other tasks remain undone.

A similar kind of passionate yearning for highbrow-oriented legitimate culture can be found also in the realm of physical participation, as attested, for instance, by stories of Eki, a 53-year-old unemployed carpenter interviewed as part of Focus Group 5 regarding his time as an amateur musician, and Karla, a 40-year-old masseuse on maternity leave about her visits to the highly legitimate Kaustinen Folk Music Festival:

> Eki: Yeah, it brings a smile to my face (…) if start dancing, and if by dancing I make other folks dance unasked, that's so much fun. When that feeling

rises... Making the feeling rise is the best thing. You don't think, like, 'what am I doing here', it's just that you manage to unite the group and you get this communal feeling that damn, this is a hell of a lot of fun.

Karla: That feeling is really so nice. There are marvellous performances, it can happen that first a live orchestra plays, then a choir sings and dancers dance these kind of folk dances (...) then there are community concerts, I was looking with my mouth open, like, 'Is this real?', as I thought there are only community singing events. Then there is a community concert in which you go with your instrument, they tell you what song they are play-ing, you have the notes there and then you just join in with your own instru-ment, it has all these kinds of nice things.

Highbrow-Oriented Cultural Participation in Surprising Places: Case Henrik

Henrik, 68, has agreed to talk to me in the meeting space of the main library of his town after seriously considering cancelling the inter-view, because he feared he would have 'nothing to say about culture'. Henrik has lots of free time now that he is retired—he has worked long years and long hours as a traffic contractor and a bus driver, a job that has taken him all over Europe. Both his parents were farmers.

Henrik is somewhat difficult to interview because he spontane-ously jumps from one conversation topic to another: he clearly has the intention of demonstrating to me the breadth of his cultural participation patterns, which are undoubtedly very varied. Although his career has been strenuous both physically and economically, he has found the time and energy to pursue his favourite leisure activity, photography, and to drive around Europe accompanying his two children—both of whom actively play classical music since a very young age—to concerts.

After retiring, Henrik has been highly active in several associa-tions, which mostly have to do with either vehicles or his personal health condition, and has organised several events and met many people. He also volunteers in a helpline for people with problems and participates in a certain kind of local resident activism that opposes changes in his neighbourhood. Henrik also loves going to flea markets and finding rare collectors' items: he is after certain extremely rare scale model cars as well as some poetry books that are

(*continued*)

(continued)

still missing in his collection. This surprising turn leads him to speak eloquently about classical literature: he is, for instance, a deep admirer of the classical Finnish poets Aleksis Kivi and Eino Leino, and he starts reciting Leino's poem *Hymyilevä Apollo* in the middle of the interview. Regarding classical cultural participation, Henrik has actively visited museums, theatres, art exhibitions and operas, mostly through his work as an organised tour bus driver but also out of interest. He regularly listens to classical music and the concerts of the Radio Symphonic Orchestra.

Henrik is a great example of the strong foothold that the Finnish working classes have in at least some traditional highbrow cultural activities and of a certain sense of ownership of legitimate culture in general. Although Henrik comes from a thoroughly working-class milieu, he does not feel particularly out of place in opera houses or theatres and skilfully navigates the cultural milieus of both bus drivers and museumgoers. In this sense, Henrik could be considered a good example of the perseverance of egalitarianism in the Finnish society. Like the working-class people interviewed by Skarpenes (2021), he feels a certain ownership of the Nordic model, clearly considers the culture of the middle or upper classes anti-hierarchical and refrains from drawing boundaries 'towards others based on culture, education, and status' (2021, 169).

A logical next step after discussing the ideal of activity is to talk about everyday participation. As we saw in Chap. 3, the debates over everyday participation depart from the idea that our perceptions of culture are, in general, too narrow and that different kinds of common, ordinary, local and mundane phenomena should be recognised as belonging to the sphere of culture (Back 2015; Ebrey 2016; Miles and Gibson 2016; Williams 1963/1971). In my data, there is indeed plenty of talk on different forms of everyday participation—such as meeting friends, socialising with neighbours, taking care of grandchildren, going to the pub, playing cards or puzzles, joining associations and so on. While large amounts of cultural and everyday participation often tend to go hand in hand (as we have seen in the cases of, for instance, Alma and Henrik), even the interviewees with very little traditional cultural participation engage in everyday participation, such as in the cases of 56-year-old unemployed Lasse and 34-year-old truck driver Petteri:

> Lasse: I almost always join these community labour events in the yard and that kind of things, and then I hang out with the blokes in the parking lot (…) I'm not overly social anymore; at some point I was the president of the committee, and then I was a bit too social, there was actually no joy in that.

> Petteri (talking about what he would typically do on a free day): Maybe I would drive around on my motorcycle, I usually always drive around a bit. Then I tinker around, I often like to tinker around in the garage and do all kinds of things, my own things. If it's really a moment when I have nothing to do and I can do what I want, then I will definitely tinker around in the garage and maybe ride on my motorbike.

Everyday participation is typically considered to be composed of informal leisure pursuits beyond narrowly defined culture (see Miles and Gibson 2016). Moreover, everyday participation was an essential part of all the tree discourses identified (affirmation, functionality and resistance): basically all interviewees engaged in activities that could be considered everyday participation. What distinguishes the everyday participation of the affirmation discourse from all others is its heavy emphasis on the importance of *being active*.

SPECIALISATIONS

A recurring finding in the data was that many people had enormous expertise in relatively small and specialised fields of culture. Interviewees willingly told me about sometimes extremely detailed cultural practices, such as where to buy the best vendace and how to fry it, how to differentiate between the many different subgenres of heavy metal based on their bottom melodies, how to understand the finesses of certain video games, or how to disassemble a vintage Chevrolet and put it back together again. These narratives are sometimes framed as a savvy way of saving money or as valuable skills in certain social circles, but mostly as an inherent pleasure of being intelligent and worthy. I interpret this as a certain 'knowing mode of cultural capital' (Prieur and Savage 2013) in which knowing something—instead of merely consuming it—becomes an important part of the appropriation of culture. Blasius and Friedrichs (2003) have argued that different kinds of practical skills, or 'a knowledge of practical life' (2003,

6), such as child-minding, gardening or fixing cars, could be understood as forms of cultural capital simply because, in theory, they could be converted into social or economic capital.

A good example of an enormously specialised form of cultural knowledge that is partly converted into social and economic capital comes from the 37-year-old cook Sami who has, in addition to his job and many other hobbies, started brewing different types of then fashionable beers such as IPAs, APAs and saisons, which have been largely unavailable in the pubs and bars of the eastern Finland city in which he lives. At the time of the interview, Sami even sells some batches of his beer to a local pub. It is noteworthy that he draws fine boundaries downwards towards 'ordinary tap lager' and takes credit for his difficult and scientific pursuit:

> Maybe it started with the fact that I myself like to try different things. When I understood that the basic lager on tap is nothing special and started to make my own stuff, I learned that you really get what you want to do, you can obtain your own aromas and hops and all that. (…) It is, it's actually a kind of a rocket science with all this stuff of growing the yeast and all that.

Another good example of highly specialised knowledge also convertible into economic capital is Marko, a farmer who lives in a small countryside village. Even though he has a highly hostile attitude towards highbrow culture, he has brought with him to the interview a photo album with pictures of his main hobby, fixing broken cars. Marko gives me a detailed account of how the process usually goes—he buys a car that someone has deemed impossible to fix, starts investigating the case, gets spare parts through his various networks in the fields ('we borrow and sell and donate parts to each other, and help each other in renovations') and finally restores cars to their original condition. He proudly shows photos of the processes and final results:

> Yeah. Then I made here this kind of adjustment thing… (..) You put here these kinds of adjustment pieces and then you have continuously variable transmission to adjust ground clearance. You can raise or lower it. You are not allowed to do this yourself because the structures of the chassis are not allowed to be welded. Our local car inspector asked me, 'Oh yeah, you have this regulation shaft here, did you buy it ready-made or did you do it yourself?'. I said, 'Well what do you think'. In those times, a ready-made regulation shaft cost 1300 markkas, but with one hundred markkas you could get these adjustment pieces. It took me (…) one hour and something. So, of

course, I did it, it was easy. (...) Then I sold it, a good five years ago, I sold it. (...) Everything worked. After standing there for nine years, I put the battery in place and filled the tank. The car started. Everything worked. Even the old radio started to sing.

Niche Activities as a Means of Distinction: Case Emilia
Emilia, a 21-year-old unemployed electrician, suggests meeting me at a local landmark bakery in a city in the north of Finland. Determined and witty, she is extremely willing to be interviewed and waits for me at the café well before our scheduled time, ordering tea and a piece of cake when I arrive.

After finishing compulsory education in the south of Finland, Emilia has enrolled in a vocational school to become an electrician. After graduating she moved to the north of Finland to work in a large international manufacturing company but was fired some months ago for reasons related to her agency contract worker status. She maintains contact with her old workmates and wishes that at some moment she could be hired again to the same job, which she really enjoyed.

Emilia likes to read and cook, but besides that she has very few highbrow-oriented activities. She does not claim to directly dislike them, but rather laments that there are very few occasions to go to events such as concerts in the city where she lives. Meanwhile, Emilia has several distinctive niche activities: as a teenager, she became a disco DJ after learning to handle the technology and travelled to many events with her record case to play, actively looking for new music. After getting her driver's licence and moving to the city in which she now lives, she has become an aficionado of the local practice of cruising with cars and now possesses extreme knowledge of both the social and technical aspects of the practice. There is, for instance, an important choreography in how the cars have to circulate in the local market square and how the cars should be eventually parked when people from a certain car want to open their windows to talk with fellow cruisers. From Emilia's group of friends, her role is usually to be the driver—she takes pride in not getting drunk and mentions with content the tradition that the passengers of the cruising car always pay the driver's cover charges at the nightclub. Emilia's

(continued)

(continued)

car is the apple of her eye: she tinkers with it often and is especially knowledgeable about its sound system, spending lots of money on expensive materials such as sounding sheets and top-notch subwoofers. She is highly critical of the mass of ignorant people who do not take care to soundproof their cars and explains in meticulous detail how it should be done.

Emilia's case is a good reminder of the fact that while traditional highbrow cultural participation might be very low, people's lives can be filled with meaningful activities involving high levels of specialisation and knowledge, and also a large amount of micro boundaries, drawn against people not 'in the know'. This attitude could be interpreted as a 'technical capital' Bourdieu speaks of (2005, 78–81), consisting of both vocational forms of education and the family inheritance of technical and practical skills.

Harnessing and putting into use these kinds of technical skills showcased above are a sign of both affirmation of the legitimacy of culture and the importance of being active, regardless of how activity is defined. In addition to being signs of a 'technical capital' (Bourdieu 2005, 78–81), they could be considered a certain kind of 'artification' or attempted legitimisation of initially popular practices. For instance, tattoo-making has been studied from this point of view of procuring cultural legitimacy to a field of culture traditionally understood as lowbrow (Kosut 2014); in the interviewed tattoo artists' discourses, there was intent to transform the symbolic valuation of tattooing and to introduce into the field fine art ideologies such as creativity and exclusiveness. What is apparent in my interviewees close to the affirmation discourse is their attitude towards participation in practical tasks: they emphasise the ideals of industriousness and devotion, as well as the possibility of some economic provisioning instead of, for instance, leisure or relax—reflecting here, for instance, the work of Moisio et al. (2013), who, comparing different types of DIY work, distinguished between the high-cultural-capital men who emphasised the autotherapeutic and leisurely aspect of housemaking and the low-cultural-capital men who considered themselves work-oriented 'handymen' with a highly regarded idea of providing for the family through labour. Finally, these (initially) working-class skills with an emphasis on a sovereign mastery of technical details can also be interpreted as displays of self-reliance, perseverance and skills of adaptation, as well as potentially handy convertibility into labour market value, in short, of a certain work ethic and certainly an attempt to create worth (Lamont 2018).

GETTING THERE: CULTURAL GOODWILL

Bourdieu famously coined his concept of cultural goodwill as an attitude born from the concern of the resource-low lower middle classes to hide their cultural ignorance and to show their docile attitudes and, at the same time, to distinguish themselves from the lower classes perceived as vulgar. As Bourdieu formulates it in the chapter on cultural goodwill in *Distinction*, '(O)ne of the surest indications of the recognition of legitimacy is the tendency of the most deprived respondents to disguise their ignorance or their indifference and to pay homage to the cultural legitimacy which the interviewer possesses in their eyes' (Bourdieu 1984/1979, 318). Later he goes on to define different forms of cultural goodwill: 'Cultural goodwill is expressed, inter alia, in a particularly frequent choice of the most unconditional testimonies of cultural docility (the choice of "well-bred" friends, a taste for "educational" or "instructive" entertainments), often combined with a sense of unworthiness ("paintings are nice but difficult")' (Bourdieu 1984/1979, 321).

Echoes of this kind of cultural goodwill were plentiful in the data, and they constituted a central part of the affirmation discourse. In the face of a 'lack' of a more codified or highbrow-oriented cultural participation from the point of view of the interviewees themselves, the core of the affirmation discourse was a lamentation of not participating in highbrow-oriented culture. Typically no specific reasons were offered; it seems that an essential part of the discourse was to simply recognise a 'fault' and to express interest in participating while consciously maintaining the status quo. There was also a clear hierarchy of cultural practices: the consumption of TV and the use of the internet and mobile phones was typically discussed as 'excessive', while reading and attending highbrow cultural events was something to be done 'more'. A good example regarding reading comes from 28-year-old Laura, a bus driver and a single mother of a small child:

> When I was a child and an adolescent I read a lot, I always received lots of books for Christmas. In some way, it's a pity that it was left behind, I should just become more active in that field (…) I don't find enough time for that, I would like to read, but I can honestly say that I only read at most two books per year (…) it's regrettable. Last year we went to Greece with my

kid, he knows how to swim and knew already then, there was a rather small pool, he was swimming and I was on the poolside reading a book and that was wonderful, I find that it empties the mind much better than browsing the phone. I would like to read, but I just can't find the moment.

The 28-year-old Sebastian, who has no formal education nor job, does not participate in highbrow culture much, but he does not oppose to it in any way, on the contrary: 'I don't go to the theatre, but I would like to. The same goes for museums, I am interested.' Maria, a 47-year-old nurse, is interested in almost anything that is mentioned in the interview: she would like to go to more classical music concerts or to furnish her house a little better. She would also like to retake the piano studies she started as a child and to study something new in general:

> I have been dreaming that it would be nice to learn. (…) One could go somewhere still as an adult, somewhere to study. But it would mean a regular thing that you attend on a regular basis. (…) I have masses of daydreams about all kinds of hobbies that I would like to take up and learn.

A very similar case is Heidi, a 26-year-old practical nurse:

> RH: What about opera?
> Heidi: I would like to go but I have not kind of gotten around to doing it, I would be incredibly interested, but…
> RH: What interests you especially?
> Heidi: Probably it's because I've never been, I don't know how the story proceeds and how they move the story along using their own voices. So kind of, I am very curious to know how the opera, how it proceeds.

According to Bourdieu's formulation, '(t)aste is an acquired disposition to "differentiate" and "appreciate"' (Bourdieu 1984/1979, 466). In relation to Heidi's argument above, a recurrent finding related to cultural capital is the enormous will of many interviewees to 'learn' more about (again, highbrow-oriented) cultural participation. In general, the affirmation discourse is laden with different kinds of attempts to adopt to 'new' or 'difficult' kinds of cultural practices which are typically discussed in an excited and docile manner. A good example is 39-year-old Ester who left her studies at the university after getting married to a medical doctor and who has since then worked in a local store. Throughout the interview, Ester describes how profoundly her husband has moulded her cultural practices regarding, for instance, music (the husband has introduced her to new genres and takes care of the children's musical education), books (the husband's father provides books), visual arts (the husband's brother is an artist) and television (the husband lightly criticises the reality shows that Ester and the children watch). Ester does recognise that the differences in their cultural practices stem from inequal social positions ('one thing is that Hannu has read his whole life, we have pretty different starting points, while we were rooting out carrots [laughs] he was reading and playing the oboe'). These differences are perhaps best crystallised in Ester's account of eating, in which she portrays herself as a picky and difficult person and the husband, along with the children, as the ones doing the right things:

RH: Any foods you hate?
    Ester: Pretty many. I have some limitations with food (laughs) kind of, when I was a child, we had potatoes and gravy, that kind of basic, country-side... And then Hannu is like, 'Don't you have the courage to try?' (...) Take for instance roe, they say that there is nothing better than roe; well, if it looks like it does [laughs] unfortunately I just cannot eat it. So, regarding bravery, I am the loser of the family (...) I'm like, maybe I could practice a bit. It's just such a strong feeling, I'm afraid that it's like... But these guys, Hannu and the children, they even taste escargots and munch wasabi nuts straight from the pack. They are like that, open-minded.

Aiming to Understand the Highbrow Sphere: Case Minna
I recruit the 38-year-old Minna through a Facebook group of family mothers, and we meet at a café of a big shopping mall by one of the ring roads of Helsinki. She refuses to have anything I offer from the café menu because she says she is on a strict diet.

Minna is an extremely talkative interviewee and is, in fact, so enthusiastic about the interview that she wants me to interview her machine operator husband as well. Minna willingly shares her life story with me: after finishing compulsory education, she quit high school and started working in different kinds of manual jobs: supermarkets, storehouses and so on. She is currently on parental leave from her factory work in a large company that forces her to be in contact with employees much higher in the hierarchy; the often-demeaning attitude of the personnel above her annoys Minna, and recently she has started dreaming of studying something else to get a different job.

(*continued*)

(continued)

Despite the many background factors predicting low cultural participation, Minna is rather active: she has had many hobbies as a child (dancing and ice skating), and currently she is busy with, for instance, American vintage cars (she and her husband often dress up, prepare their 1950s' vehicle and meet other enthusiasts) and with taking her child to different activities (music, painting and swimming). In addition, she loves museums, rock concerts and fairs. What is interesting in Minna's story is that although she does not regularly attend the most highbrow forms of cultural participation, such as opera or ballet, she would *really* like to—in fact, she and her husband have actively tried to attend such events in order to understand more about them. Minna's explanation is worth quoting at length:

> I told my husband that in the name of general education: should we go once to the ballet and once to the opera? We went to the ballet… It was many years ago, but we dressed nicely and got ourselves a box and all that and well, my husband fell asleep and I tried, I really tried, I had like opened all of my senses to the ballet, but I could not get a grip of it. (…RH: What was it, why couldn't you get a grip?) I don't understand. It just did not address me. They danced so nicely, but… I could not get a hold of it, I was as open as I could, I concentrated, I listened, I really sensitised myself to the performance, but it was not my thing at all. I could not get a grip of it at all.

Minna's attitude reflects well that participating in (highbrow) culture is not just a question of will or the right attitude: it is also a question of long-term exposure, familiarity and education, in short, of an embodied capacity to extract meaning or pleasure from cultural participation. Her case is a good example of what Bourdieu meant when referring to the cultural disposition of being able to decipher certain forms of culture: 'Since the information presented by the works exhibited exceeds the deciphering capacities of the beholder, he perceives them as devoid of signification – or, to be more precise, of structuration and organization – because he cannot "decode" them, i.e. reduce them to an intelligible form' (Bourdieu 1993, 217). Bourdieu continues that the satisfaction extracted from certain cultural practices is attached to the 'right' kind of cultural disposition and remains 'only accessible to those who are disposed to appropriate them because they attribute a value to them' (1993, 227).

Another aspect of the presence of cultural goodwill in the data and in the affirmation discourse was the emphasis that many interviewees placed on their children 'inheriting' desirable patterns of cultural practices. We know from the previous chapters that the intergenerational transmission of cultural practices works in such a way that highly educated parents' children participate in culture the most (van Hek and Kraaykamp 2013; Kallunki and Purhonen 2017). What is more, different 'enrichment activities' for children constitute an important part of nudging children into a middle-class context (Lareau 2011; Vincent and Ball 2007). These many burdens of ensuring that a child is comfortable in middle-class settings were extremely noticeable in the interviews. Linda, a 30-year-old student on maternity leave (who is herself very active both regarding both highbrow-oriented cultural participation and everyday participation), coins this desire well as striving for 'naturalness':

(Speaking of museums): …I think it's anyway a good habit that you know how to visit museums and understand things and in that way gather a bit of information on history. I try to educate in a way that [my child] would know how to… Or that this kind of environment would feel natural even when he grows up.

A similar urge to encourage the cultural participation of children is found also in the most deprivileged social strata of the interviews. For instance, Eeva, the retired nurse cited earlier in this chapter, speaks directly of 'nudging' her two children towards musical hobbies (an effort that proved to be successful, as both children went through prestigious musical academies). The 43-year-old Kimmo, who is simultaneously unemployed, on disability pension and going through a process of debt adjustment, describes taking his young child to the musical conservatory as his main priority, discussing the possible future gains of the hobby in what can be interpreted as a middle-class terminology:

I have this outlook that it kind of develops social skills and all kinds of other skills beyond just the playing… It boosts your self-esteem as it now includes live performances and that kind of stuff. So not only for playing the instrument… at least that's my outlook.

In addition to music, reading was again mentioned as an important asset for the children—children 'should' be taken to libraries and read aloud to, and later they should be 'forced' to read. For instance, Aleksi, a 29-year-old sports instructor on parental leave, has adopted a quasi-technical attitude towards his toddler's reading habits; he takes the child to the library once a week to spend two or three hours and reads to him aloud ('even two and a half hours per day'). A very similar attitude was exhibited by many (especially female) interviewees who lamented that their small children read books or visited the library too seldom:

> Minna (talking about library visits): Too seldom, we should go more. I think the boy has never visited the library even if (…) we have it within just a couple of kilometers. We should do it, I just haven't gotten around to doing it. Even if we read a lot as we have many children's books, we read them but… (…) I feel now as if I am, not a bad mother or anything, but I mean that I have not taken my child to the library, so what the hell, should I do it? But that's it, I would like to visit it more (Minna, 38, manual worker)

> Laura (talking about her son reading): …I should encourage him that 'Hey, choose yourself any book', I don't mean a hundred-page book, something small, and 'Now you will read this book during this week', you know, some-thing like that, I do argue that in the present-day world these mobile phones (…) I should encourage my own boy to do that, like 'Hey, read'. Probably our brain works differently when we read.
> (Laura, 28, bus driver)

In the same style but in a different direction, significant others, such as spouses and other family members, have often altered the interviewees' cultural participation practices in significant ways; in the affirmation dis-course, this is always discussed as an exciting and positive opportunity that broadens one's horizons, for instance, 34-year-old truck driver Petteri, who has become an avid reader thanks to the books that his cousin pro-vides him, and the 47-year-old nurse Maria, whose adult children have sparked her interest in theatre and musicals and who now loves different live shows: 'My daughter took me to London to see *Les Misérables*. That was such an experience that I think nothing will ever thrill me in the same way'. Besides Ester, whom we know from above, the best example of a higher-educated spouse's effects regarding an increase in a partner's cul-tural participation (and knowledge) comes from Aleksi, a 29-year-old sports instructor who is on parental leave—and whose wife has tertiary education. With a genuine smile, Aleksi tells me that his wife has set spe-cific targets to make him participate more in culture. For instance, when they go on trips, they have made an interesting agreement:

Me and my spouse actually have this kind of deal regarding museums as we travel a lot, for instance now we just came home from Prague: we do one museum and then one bar. That makes one museum, one beer, one museum, one beer [laughs]. I'm not a kind of museum person myself, I like this kind of natural history museums and museums that have these kinds of interactive exhibitions. I've never been a museum visitor who would have the energy to read any texts. Somehow, I willingly join, I have nothing against it, but if I got to choose, I would not choose going to a museum.

We have seen that the cultural goodwill firmly present in the affirmation discourse is composed of surprisingly similar elements than Bourdieu's theory of cultural goodwill: it includes an aspiration to accept and adapt to the perceived upper-class cultural practices (classical music, ballet, museums and so on). Many interviewees emphasised their positive attitude towards highbrow-oriented cultural participation and stressed their willingness to learn and to make their possible children acquainted to it. This resonates with Bourdieu's original idea that 'the different social classes differ not so much in the extent to which they acknowledge culture as in the extent to which they know it' (Bourdieu 1984/1979, 318).

Cautious Downward Boundaries

So far, the affirmation discourse has involved mainly positive and docile tones: the consecration of cultural participation as something with intrinsic value, something that 'should' be done. This attitude is further reflected in the cautious downward boundaries that are an essential part of the affirmation discourse. The objects of these boundaries are the usual suspects of 'bad taste'—in other words, entertainment-oriented or extremely commercial television programmes and different kinds of tabloids and scandal newspapers, all associated with lower-class tastes both in the public imaginary and according to existing research (Purhonen et al. 2014; Taylor 2016).

In the affirmation discourse, television in general is criticised as a distraction from more meaningful forms of cultural participation, with most people stating that they watch 'all too much'. As 30-year-old student Linda coins it: 'We barely watch TV (...) what somehow disgusts me about TV is that it's so horribly time-consuming'. When considering in more detail why television is so bad, many interviewees mention particular genres such as comedy (something that 'comes with the laughs on', as

59-year-old pensioner Hely puts it) and reality television shows (the truck driver Petteri, 34, is horrified that his wife watches *Temptation Island*: 'I cannot understand the idea, I don't get it. I just don't understand').

In some of the critical accounts of television, strong moral boundaries are drawn. The discourses surrounding them remind of the middle-class voices found in the study by Skeggs et al. (2008) that took critical distance to reality television and its 'inauthentic' working-class participants. A good example is the discussion in the Focus Group 3 with a retired couple with vocational school education and their adult daughter, a childminder on parental leave:

> Malla: My most hated thing are these reality TV shows, whatever dating things they put, paradise islands and hotels and whatever... I never watch them.
> RH: What feels repulsive about them?
> Malla: Nah, they are in some way so artificial and...
> Esko: Yes, they fake it.
> Malla: .....yes, it's a kind of a trivial nonsense, nah, somehow it does not amuse me at all.
> Elina: It's not real in any way.
> (...)
> Malla: These cooking programmes in particular are so horrible, I'm not interested.
> Esko: Some *Australian MasterChef*, you're like, 'What the hell'.
> Malla: Who is interested in someone that fries a steak there? No, those programmes are never watched in our house. Neither these kinds of *Emmerdale* and *The Bold and the Beautiful*... we don't watch these kinds of soap operas.

A similar but edgier opinion is given by Marko, a farmer with no formal education:

> Marko (on bad TV programmes): Nowadays you get at least ten channels all day long, and most of it is pure shit that you can't even watch. (...) These soap operas are something that I can't be bothered to watch. The bold and the beautiful and the fat and the ugly and whatever there is.

Another genre treated in the affirmation discourse with nearly the same contempt as television and discussed through downward boundaries involved tabloids and scandal newspapers, sometimes also different light literature genres which were condemned as 'useless rubbish'. 'I am not interested in these kinds of nonsense books – I don't know that literary genre but I can guess more or less what it is about', says Timo, 51-year-old farmer from Focus Group 9. Regarding gossip magazines, the tip of iceberg for drawing boundaries is found in their morally dubious character:

> I don't understand its stories [laughs], they are kind of... No, no, that's not my kind of magazine. (...) All this kind of 'This celebrity did this and this celebrity did that', I find it unnecessary.
> (Kaisa, 54, ward domestic)

> RH: What annoys you about it [gossip magazine *Seitsemän päivää*, or *Seven days*])?
> Sami: Mostly the news. It's not valid information in any way. If I want to read fictive stuff, I will get myself a book based on that genre. If I want to read articles from the newspaper, I would like them to have some kind of truth to them. I won't accept them even as humour (Sami, 37, cook)

We have earlier discussed that the affirmation discourse includes a strong ideal of activity: participating in culture, or expressing a willingness to participate, is considered the inherently right thing to do. In the affirmation discourse, this is expressed almost like a norm, which, in turn, offers the opportunity to draw boundaries against inactive people and to consider them lazy, very much as in the discursive subject identity that Stevenson found to be characteristic in the top-down blaming of non-participants as deviant (Stevenson 2019). There were echoes of this same idea throughout the data: many men described their houses or cars as projects requiring an 'endless' amount of work, whereas many women concretely drew boundaries against people who did not do anything. Good examples about the distinctive importance attributed to remaining active come from farmer's wife Salla, 43, and the student Linda, 30:

> I don't know about holidays in the sun... Just lying under the sun, well, we are not really the kind of people that just lie on the beach.

> A person has to have hobbies! If there are people who never go anywhere, I'm like, what are you doing?

It appears as if the downward boundaries drawn in the affirmation discourse are tied, apart from representing an orientation of cultural goodwill, into a vague idea of middle-class respectability (Skeggs 2005): being respectable, in the mindset of these interviewees, entails adhering to the norms of appreciating and valuing highbrow-oriented cultural participation (though not necessarily participating in it) and maintaining a certain activeness in life but while shunning obvious lowbrow practices, such as watching lowbrow television.

CONCLUSION: EVERYDAY CULTURAL GOODWILL?

We have seen that the affirmation discourse is, in fact, a discourse of activity. When observed at the level of participation practices, peoples' accounts reveal that there is plenty of both traditional highbrow-oriented participation and different kinds of everyday participation. This seems to echo the scholarly finding that active participation in culture is not necessarily differentiated (only) through 'highbrow' and 'everyday' modes of participation, but that it is at least partly a question of the same people participating in both highbrow and different kinds of more mundane forms of culture (Heikkilä and Lindblom 2022).

In the affirmation discourse, the idea that participating in culture is 'good for you' is taken very seriously. Culture is attributed to an unquestionable intrinsic value: it is largely thought that participating in culture will bring about well-being and social integration (see Milling 2019). It could be interpreted that the affirmation discourse still has confidence in the power of cultural participation to function as a mechanism for providing cultural capital (Lamont and Lareau 1988).

In the affirmation discourse, the only boundaries drawn are drawn downwards. They basically only have aesthetic content and touch upon the most classical items of popular lowbrow taste, such as reality television, the yellow press and so on (cf. Skeggs et al. 2008). These few careful moral downward boundaries are directed against 'laziness' or people 'not doing anything'; in other words, in the affirmation discourse, there seems to be an inherent idea of adjusting to the hegemonic discourse whereby one must participate in culture.

The affirmation discourse is marked by significant affinity, excitement, favourableness and positivity towards cultural participation: a certain 'reflexive appropriation' 'in a spirit of openness' (Bennett et al. 2009, 194). In other words, this discourse reflects in many ways many middle-class values and ideals—a 'desire to pass as middle class' (Skeggs 1997, 91). Bourdieu himself argued that the cultural goodwill project of the (lower) middle classes is doomed to fail due to the misrecognition of cultural products as 'higher' than they actually are—this is why people would accept '"sparkling white wine" for champagne, imitation leather for real leather, reproductions for paintings' and so on (Bourdieu 1984/1979, 386). In the case of the affirmation discourse, instead of the cultural good-will coined by Bourdieu, we could perhaps speak of an '*everyday* cultural goodwill'—the affirmation discourse approaches general activity, made up of both highbrow-oriented and everyday participation, as a token of their compliant and submissive attitudes, as well as a means of distinguishing oneself from the groups perceived as vulgar and located lower on the social ladder, not only due to their lowbrow cultural practices but also because of a deplorable and non-distinctive 'laziness', a logical opposition to the vigorous and perky self-image offered by the affirmation discourse.

How does all this translate into an egalitarian context such as Finland? De Keere (2020) has argued that when moral positions are studied as both class and status markers and endeavours to gain worth, egalitarianism is actually found in the area of low overall resources and an emphasis on cultural (instead of economic) capital. In this sense, the affirmation discourse thoroughly characterises the egalitarian worldviews of conformity and ideals of high collective interference. It could be argued that it is a certain sign of egalitarianism that people from rather unprivileged back-grounds so strongly take 'ownership' of highbrow-oriented cultural participation, feel at ease reading books or visiting theatres and museums, and in general consider themselves *able and willing* to participate in culture, even if, in the end, they would not do so. We have also seen couples with diverging 'cultural baggage', which was seen not as a source of conflict but rather as a challenge with a solution. However, this is not the whole story considering the data involving unprivileged people and groups. The next empirical chapters will put these findings into context.

References

Back L (2015) Why Everyday Life Matters: Class, Community and Making Life Livable. *Sociology* 49(5): 820–836.

Bennett T, Savage M, Silva E, Warde A, Gayo-Cal M and Wright D (2009) *Culture, Class, Distinction*. London: Routledge.

Blasius J and Friedrichs J (2003) Les compétences pratiques font-elles partie du capital culturel ? *Revue française de sociologie* 44: 549–576.

Bourdieu P (1984/1979) *Distinction. A Social Critique of the Judgment of Taste*. London: Routledge & Kegan Paul.

Bourdieu P (1993) *The Field of Cultural Production. Essays on Art and Literature.* New York: Columbia Press.

Bourdieu P (2005) *The Social Structures of the Economy.* Cambridge: Polity Press.

De Keere K (2020) Finding the moral space: Rethinking morality, social class and worldviews. *Poetics* 79: 101415.

Ebrey J (2016) The mundane and insignificant, the ordinary and the extraordinary: Understanding Everyday Participation and theories of everyday life. *Cultural Trends* 25(3):158–168.

Heikkilä R and Lindblom T (2022) Overlaps and accumulations: The anatomy of cultural non-participation in Finland, 2007 to 2018. *Journal of Consumer Culture.* Available at: https://doi.org/10.1177/14695405211062052 (Accessed 21 August 2022).

Itkonen J (2009). Juoksuaika. [Time to run.] *Apu* 8/2009. Available at: https://www.apu.fi/artikkelit/juoksuaika (Accessed 21 August 2022).

Kallunki J and Purhonen S (2017) Intergenerational transmission of cultural capital in Finland. *Research on Finnish Society* 10: 101–111.

Kosut M (2014) The Artification of Tattoo: Transformations within a Cultural Field. *Cultural Sociology* 8(2): 142–158.

Lamont M (2018) Addressing Recognition Gaps: Destigmatization and the Reduction of Inequality. *American Sociological Review* 83(3): 419–444.

Lamont M and Lareau A (1988) Cultural capital: Allusions, gaps and glissandos in recent theoretical developments. *Sociological theory* 153–168.

Lareau A (2011) *Unequal Childhoods. Class, Race, and Family Life.* Berkeley: University of California Press.

Miles A and Gibson L (2016) Everyday participation and cultural value. *Cultural Trends* 25(3): 151–157.

Milling J (2019) Valuing cultural participation: The usefulness of the eighteenth-century stage. In: Belfiore E and Gibson L (eds) *Histories of Cultural Participation, Values and Governance.* London: Palgrave Macmillan, pp. 17–41.

Moisio R, Arnould EJ and Gentry JW (2013) Productive Consumption in the Class-Mediated Construction of Domestic Masculinity: Do-It-Yourself (DIY) Home Improvement in Men's Identity Work. *Journal of Consumer Research* 40(2): 298–316.

Prieur A and Savage M (2013) Emerging forms of cultural capital. *European Societies* 15(2): 246–267.

Purhonen S, Gronow J, Heikkilä R, Kahma N, Rahkonen K, Toikka A (2014) *Suomalainen maku: Kulttuuripääoma, kulutus ja elämäntyylien sosiaalinen eriytyminen [Finnish taste: Cultural capital, consumption and the social differentiation of lifestyles].* Helsinki: Gaudeamus.

Rosa H (2013) *Social Acceleration. A New Theory of Modernity.* Columbia: Columbia University Press.

Skarpenes O (2021) Defending the Nordic model: Understanding the moral universe of the Norwegian working class. *European Journal of Cultural and Political Sociology* 8(2): 151–174.

Skeggs B (1997) *Formations of Class and Gender. Becoming respectable.* London: Sage.

Skeggs B (2005) The Making of Class and Gender through Visualizing Moral Subject Formation. *Sociology* 39(5): 965–982.

Skeggs B, Wood H and Thumim N (2008) Oh goodness I am watching reality TV: How methods make class in audience research. *European Journal of Cultural Studies* 11(1): 5–24.

Stevenson D (2019) The cultural non-participant: Critical logics and discursive subject identities. *Arts and the Market* 9(1): 50–64.

Sullivan O (2008) Busyness, Status Distinction and Consumption Strategies of the Income Rich, Time Poor. *Time & Society* 17(1): 5–26.

Taylor M (2016) Nonparticipation or Different styles of Participation? Alternative Interpretations from Taking Part. *Cultural Trends* 25(3): 169–181.

van Hek M and Kraaykamp G (2013) Cultural Consumption across Countries: A Multi-level Analysis of Social Inequality in Highbrow Culture in Europe. *Poetics* 41(4): 323–341.

Vincent C and Ball SJ (2007) "Making up" the middle-class child: Families, activities and class dispositions. *Sociology* 41(6): 1061–1077.

Weingartner S and Rössel J (2019) Changing dimensions of cultural consumption? The space of lifestyles in Switzerland from 1976 to 2013. *Poetics* 74: 101345.

Williams R (1963/1971) *Culture and society (1780–1950).* London: Pelican.

CHAPTER 6

Functionality

Abstract This chapter focuses on the second out of three discourses found in the data. Within this 'functionality discourse', there is mainly popular and everyday participation. This discourse emphasises the practical usefulness of cultural practices: it is an area of personal 'feelgood'. The functionality discourse is marked by a link between cultural participation and the structuring factors of life. At the same time, cultural participation is rarely conceived of as culturally distinctive. There is an emphasis on modesty, but the boundaries drawn are aesthetical and directed upwards towards impractical cultural practices. In other words, in the functionality discourse, there are delicate traces of anti-elitism. This indifferent and self-assured attitude towards cultural participation that characterises the functionality discourse could be considered a version of egalitarianism.

Keywords Functionality discourse • Modesty • Sense of one's place • Upward symbolic boundaries • Egalitarianism

© The Author(s) 2022, corrected publication 2023   89
R. Heikkilä, *Understanding Cultural Non-Participation in an Egalitarian Context*, Palgrave Studies in Cultural Participation,
https://doi.org/10.1007/978-3-031-18865-7_6

PROLOGUE

Maarit, 37, lives alone in a studio in a laid-back, diverse and heavily gentri-
fied urban area of Helsinki. We meet at a seaside café, and Maarit orders a
piece of raw cake. Maarit is a willing and reflexive interviewee who laughs
a lot at her own cultural practices.

After finishing high school, Maarit first worked abroad as an au pair for
some years. After returning to Finland, she worked for several years in a
warehouse while trying to make it into the polytechnic university and the
university, but as those doors never opened for her, she studied to become
a practical nurse. She has now started to study physiotherapy at a polytechnic university outside of Helsinki and works some hours every week as a
personal assistant.

Maarit's free time is characterised by activities such as yoga, hydrospin-
ning and going to concerts (mostly of different kinds of spiritual artists,
but occasionally even rap). Although she very little money, Maarit sees it
as a conscious choice that she left the well-paid warehouse job and settled
for a life with less money but more quality ('Now that I consciously work
very little, I've had very little money to have holidays or travel anywhere').
Maarit is extremely social both with family and friends—she tells an anec-
dote about becoming good friends with a neighbour after losing the key
to her flat when wearing only a bathrobe in her staircase. Currently, studying and working have made her time very scarce, so she also needs wind-
ing down ('I need lots of time to load my batteries'). On many occasions,
Maarit speaks of 'resetting herself to zero': she likes to do things that
require minimum effort and that relax her. A good example is that she
reads a lot, but admits mostly reading the same books over and over again,
namely, the Harry Potter series and Jane Austen's works, which she calls
'comfort reading' ('I know beforehand how it is, it's so relaxing because I
don't have to even concentrate when I read'). After occasionally going
outside of a certain emotional safe space, for instance, when trying to read
author Sofi Oksanen's prize-winning novel *Purge* on the Soviet occupation of Estonia, Maarit came to the conclusion that she does not want to
force herself beyond her comfort zone ('I had to leave it unfinished,
because it was so disturbing, I felt so bad ... It might be a book that everyone should read, but I don't have to... I consciously don't want to cause
myself that').

Maarit describes her whole cultural practices as being traversed by a
demand for easy choices and feelgood ('I am this kind of instant

gratification kind of person. So, I guess that affects my choices'). For instance, when listening to music, Maarit mostly chooses things that fit her mood ('I think that with the help of music you can... for instance, dismantle aggressivity; if for some reason you feel aggressive, then you listen to aggressive music. But mostly I like to use music in a way that I soften the feeling by listening to music that makes you feel good, for instance something really sunny... That inevitably makes you smile'). When she cannot sleep, she calms herself down with kundalini music and stresses the importance of not being able to follow the lyrics: 'The lyrics are in a language that I don't understand, which relaxes me'.

The few boundaries Maarit draws are directed downwards towards things such as horror movies and violence, which make her feel bad, reality television ('I think they are a bit of empty entertainment that stem from other peoples' stupidities') and the yellow press ('I hate clickbait headlines'). She conceives them all as not fitting *her*—that is, someone else might find them interesting or useful.

Maarit's lifestyle is probably a very typical example of a young and urban cultural practices palette: very little highbrow-oriented participation, some popular and everyday participation and, in general, a highly open-minded and tolerant attitude towards others' cultural practices. What makes her case a good introduction to the functionality discourse is that she speaks of all of her cultural participation in a self-referential manner: she consumes things that makes her feel good and lift her mood as needed. This is a way of breaking free from the bonds of cultural capital— in short, of making cultural participation a question of functionality.

ESCAPES FROM REALITY

Maarit's case above is a good example of the functionality discourse, first of all because cultural participation (or the 'lack' of it) is not presented as a factor that could enable distinction or the accumulation of cultural capital and, second, because functionality takes place in the interviews typically as an emphasis on individuality. In other words, cultural participation is not a game that is played on a common field, but an individual process in which certain items are cherry-picked for oneself in order to cater to some specific need or material condition. Different from the affirmation discourse, in which the importance of cultural participation was considered to have intrinsic value, in the functionality discourse the material side of cultural participation is always present. Most typically it has to do with the

difficult integration of cultural participation and work. The finding of
Miles and Sullivan (2012) that shift workers are typically shut out from
cultural participation is recurrent in my data: many interviewees with difficult working hours found themselves permanently tired and exhausted,
due to both physically strenuous work and family obligations. For instance,
Mimosa, a 37-year-old cleaner who only works night shifts, is permanently
so tired that after going to the gym and having a shower in the morning
after her shift is over, she is only able to rest:

> I rest, I listen to music, if my boyfriend is not home, I enjoy the feeling of
> silence around me. Sometimes I have days in which I only want to be in that
> bubble of silence, I won't turn anything on, not even the television.

A highly similar case is that of 54-year-old ward domestic Kaisa, who
has all the potential to be a heavy user of culture ('I'm an avid reader, I'm
a large-scale consumer of the library, and also I go the cultural house for
concerts'): she admits being so tired that she is not able to do much during the weekends:

> Now I am dreaming of starting a job alternation leave at the end of the year.
> I have been asking for permission and I have been conceded a leave, they
> have found someone to cover for me. Now that I am beginning to feel my
> age, I want to do something that I really wish, because weekends just go by
> with me feeling like… Nowadays, I get really tired at work because it's all
> the time this kind of physical lifting and so on. So now I have this dream. Of
> course I have enough free time, evenings and so on, but if you are tired, you
> just don't have the energy.

What links this permanent exhaustion of the unprivileged groups to the
functionality discourse is their presentation of cultural participation as an
alternative or as an *escape* from the tedious routine and the hardships of
everyday life. For instance, Minna, the 38-year-old manual worker we met
in the previous chapter, is permanently dreaming of going away to a hotel
just to be in peace for a while. She thoroughly explains why she loves reality television so much: for her, it represents a means of getting away from
her own problems for a while. A very similar account, perhaps more from
a male perspective, is provided by the 29-year-old Aleksi, a sport instructor
on parental leave:

Minna: Temptation Island is on today. I like it because when I look at those nonsense series I can relax completely. I forget my own worries, I just live in it completely, I kind of live with those people. It's so funny, sometimes it bugs you; if people start to fight in one of those series, I get annoyed. (…) It's my thing, I watch it for one hour or one and a half hours or whatever each programme takes… that's a way for me to relax completely. It's nice.

Aleksi: You put kind of a series or movie on the television, and as I'm interested in rums, I poor myself a drink to accompany, and some nice evening snack, then you just sit and lie on the sofa and reset yourself to zero and allow your brain to be completely empty, doing nothing. Somehow I've always been a person who is really active and has many different hobbies, so in some way I've learned to notice it in myself that sometimes I have to reset myself to zero, reset my brain so it does not get overloaded.

Finding Shelter from the Everyday: Case Iina
Iina is a 45-year-old retail dealer in a small town in the north of Finland. She has invited me to the back room of her shop to do the interview and is a willing interviewee.

Iina has had a vivid educational and professional path: she is a high school dropout ('I was kind of a rough adolescent, one day I just decided that I've had enough and will break even') who left home early, worked at a restaurant, studied restauration at a polytechnic, worked at a farm after marrying a farmer ('Then I moved to the backwoods to become a farmer's wife… for fifteen years I was milking cows [laughs]') and, after divorcing, worked in network marketing and later decided to establish her own shop. This has given Iina a certain amount of freedom: although she works a lot, she has hired some employees and can go on vacation from time to time. At the moment of the interview, she had just spent one month in Vietnam with a friend. After her divorce, she has formed a reconstituted family with her current husband who works as a guard.

Iina is very sporty and goes to the gym ('four times a week, also I try to do two or three aerobic workouts'). In addition, she knits a lot ('absolutely everything, from jumpers to socks'). She listens to music all the time, mostly nineties pop ('I listen to music whenever possible, and I like to listen to it alone, you know, with earbuds in my ears. At the gym I get to be in peace as I listen to music… I listen to

(*continued*)

(continued)
music in the car and at home mostly to Spotify. That allows me to listen to the exact music I want'). Other than that, Iina has very few activities outside of work: she used to be active in associations, but has left this activity behind. The only newspaper she follows is Fit, a magazine concentrating on sports and well-being.

When discussing cultural items that she does not like, Iina seems to discover the axis of her cultural practices: she distances herself from fiction deemed too realistic, documentaries and so on, because she demands a full immersion, something that helps forget daily worries and suffering: 'And if we speak of books and TV programmes and this kind of stuff, I can't take it if it's based on reality, that sucks. It needs to have something that helps you escape this ordinary misery [laughs]'. During her recent trip to Vietnam, she saw a documentary on the Nazis, which helped her crystallise what, according to her, was wrong with documentaries: 'They are always somehow sad. Documentaries are always kind of, you know, they make you cry. On my trip I watched a documentary on the Nazis and concentration camps, it was quite interesting anyway... Maybe the thing was to see how crazy those people actually were. How was it possible that they were brainwashed to do that?' Iina reads relatively little, but mentions, for instance, Dan Brown as a writer she likes, for the same reason: 'I like Dan Brown, he is able to bind the fiction so well into the existing framework... You get this feeling that it would be actually true even if it's not. It is kind of comforting that it is not true'.

Iina embodies well the spirit of the functionality discourse; she is highly concerned with what fits *her* personally rather than what counts as good or bad taste or desirable or vulgar cultural practices. Iina's attitude could perhaps be best understood as an example of cultural practices that have only superficial ties to structural factors, such as class, and are presented as personal and individualistic (Bauman 1991; Featherstone 1991).

The approach to cultural participation as 'escapes from reality' that was shared by many interviewees can be put into context through understanding the role of entertainment in cultural participation. Levine (1988) has written that before the nineteenth century, both upper and lower classes shared a similar repertoire of available cultural items. During the nineteenth century, the elites managed to distinguish their cultural practices as 'higher' than those of the 'masses', which led to the 'sacralization of culture' (Levine 1988, 83), the process of separating high culture from entertainment. The functionality discourse involves a heavy emphasis on entertainment-oriented cultural participation, and it is framed around a conscious choice of a perfect fit and counterpoint for an active yet rough working life.

PRACTICALITY

In the functionality discourse, one interesting phenomenon is the inclusion of sports in the sphere of cultural participation. Sport is typically motivated as a practical alternative for highbrow-oriented participation—in most of the functionality discourse, sports and physical exercise are something that one does 'of course' and teaches the children to do, in a very similar way to how traditional culture was spoken about in the affirmation discourse. For instance, truck driver Petteri, 34, emphasises the value of teaching the children to do sports and explains that 'indeed we have gone skating and this kind of thing regularly, we have practiced skiing regularly'.

Although there is large variation regarding the choice of sport, practising sports has become a middle-class activity rather than a pastime of the lower-status groups, also in Finland (Kahma 2012), and the interviewees seemed to sense that mentioning being physically active would be interpreted as something positive in the interviews. In some cases, it was a shorthand for having and demonstrating resources or worth, especially in small towns with limited highbrow-oriented offerings. In some cases, practising sports through the rough seas is presented as something heroic:

Even if it was 20 degrees minus Celsius we would go to the field to play ice bandy. There were no dressing rooms. You would put your skates on in the snow, and off you went.
(Jarmo, 67, retired)

Sports seemed in general to provide a means of showing off capitals among the interviewees: in a milieu of popular and mundane cultural practices that the interviewees probably recognised as de-legitimised by the classes above them in the hierarchy (see Skeggs and Loveday 2012), practising sports was linked in the interviews to values such as perseverance, activity and self-maintenance, something many interviewees saw as a viable alternatives to simply lying around or 'staring at too many screens'. For instance, Karla, a 40-year-old masseuse on maternity leave living in a small village in the north of Finland, has very few possibilities for traditional cultural participation due to time and location restraints, at least, but she seems to compensate for this lack with a sporty attitude that resembles multitasking:

> Karla: I do as versatile sports as I can (…) Well we do a little bit of gymnastics on the floor, and then I do pram jogging, which makes me leave the house. The baby sleeps really well outside, so I purposely do a longer jog to get more oxygen. When there was less snow in the autumn, I did circuit training and checked on the baby, who was sleeping outside. If she would wake up, I would grab the pram and go jogging, and then I would continue my exercise outdoors.

The interviews include many references to the normative ideal about the many 'benefits' of cultural participation. Most interviewees recognise the positive characteristics associated with highbrow-oriented cultural participation: they mention that they would like to listen more to classical music or to do more sports because it supposedly 'relaxes you'. However, in the functionality discourse, the idea is to use cultural participation in an instrumental way for direct pleasure or fun or to get into the right kind of mood. Listening to music, in general, seems to be the one of the main outlets of the functionality of cultural participation:

> If you need a kind of boost – for instance, when you go jogging – you can play something, or if you want something relaxing, you can put one of those, I guess they call it motivational music or whatever. I've listened to music since I was a kid (…) Pink Floyd and this kind of thing (…) Queen and Moody Blues and so on, I've grown up with that.
> (Anniina, 39, unemployed salesperson)

> Jarkko: For me, music has always been a way of dealing with feelings – for instance, when I was a teenager. I listened to heavy music, if I would listen

to those songs now I would be like, Oh my god [laughs]. It's good music, but it's kind of hard to listen to, because of course it's connected to those specific teenage feelings, so in a way, I don't want to feel them again, in a way I cannot listen to it. I kind of always connect music to a specific state of mind, that's how it is.

Milla: And of course, if I start to vacuum clean, I will put some music on.

(Focus Group 4: Jarkko, 27, engineer, and Milla, 26, student at a vocational school)

In some way, music has been, for me, since the teenage years, a kind of way of relaxing or working through feelings – for instance, when I do sports, I put my earphones on my ears before an important match and listen carefully to certain songs. At home, if I'm stressed or annoyed, I listen to a certain kind of music, or if I have the feeling that I just want to enjoy the moment and listen to something good, I just lie on the floor and stare at the ceiling and listen to some specific songs.

(Aleksi, 29, sports instructor on parental leave)

One of the most concrete tokens of functionality was in this discourse related to money. In general, most of my interviewees lamented their poor economic situation—which was only logical given their background profiles. Although using the lack of money as a *reason* not to participate was more common in the affirmation discourse, the functionality discourse drew strongly on an idea of consuming culture in clever and crafty ways— making intelligent choices while also saving money and, in this way, demonstrating 'worth' in a scenario of scarcity. The Focus Group 5 with unemployed men was a clear demonstration of people's ability to adapt their cultural practices to prevailing structural constraints: the men spoke at length about their inability to order the local newspapers, the impossibility of attending concerts ('in my circles, there is often a lack of money') and their necessity to buy food with a red discount tag ('anything goes when you are hungry'). Accounts of surviving with very little money are sometimes framed as stories of resourcefulness wit, as in the following excerpt from a focus group:

Santeri: A couple of years ago I found in the paper recycling bin this kind of a meter-high pile of all kinds of books. I was taking rubbish there, I peeked in and ran quickly home to get plastic bags. Then I took them all home, and that was 50 books.

RH: What kinds of books were they?

Santeri: There were all kinds of real books. Also paperbacks, I think they call them like that. But it was nice to read them.
(Focus Group 5: Santeri, 58, unemployed teacher)

An example of a very similar discourse is found in Focus Group 4 with a young working-class couple: the entire interview revolves around the wife's stories of the different bargains she has made; even the couple's wedding rings were bought during a 50% sale, which they found to be a fantastic bargain. Many other interviewees reveal that saving money can be made an art or at least a meaningful form of cultural participation in itself:

Mimosa: Oh yeah, we will have an Easter ham, we won't be making lamb.
RH: You will have ham?
Mimosa: After Christmas ham was so cheap in Lidl that we bought three hams and put them in the freezer: that makes for an Easter ham, a May Day ham and a Midsummer ham.
(Mimosa, 37, cleaner)

Melissa: Yeah, sometimes in the summer, we might have gone to the park as the music is carried there.
RH: OK, so you go outside the festival to listen to it?
Melissa: Yeah, with my friend we sit in the park.
RH: Do you sit outside for saving money?
Melissa: Well, what's the point of paying the entrance fee? The drinks cost a lot, everything costs a lot, there is no point, you rather sit outside with some nice guys and talk and listen to the music at the same time.
(Melissa, NA, disability pensioneer)

I go jogging pretty much alone because I am a passionate saver of money. I always go to a certain shop if I see that OK, there is that kind of offer there, I go and collect it and walk at the same time, two hours is the usual thing, but, well, it's not as if I have sweat running down my forehead or anything. Then, I walk and check flea markets.
(Julia, 68, pensioner)

The demand expressed by many of my interviewees that cultural participation should perform some kind of function resonates thoroughly with Bourdieu's (highly contested) idea of the 'taste of necessity' which was originally coined as the inability of the lower classes to create proper tastes. Bourdieu held that in a scenario of limited economic resources, the cultural practices of the lower classes are always a mere 'resignation to necessity' (Bourdieu 1984/1979, 380)—this is what makes them adopt functional and useful cultural items and shun things that they consider unpractical or needless and therefore ostentatious. Blasius and Friedrichs go on to empirically assess Bourdieu's claim that members of the lower classes cannot convert economic capital into cultural capital and, in fact, find firm support for Bourdieu's original thesis (Blasius and Friedrichs 2008). Thus, the lower classes seem to be doomed to a position of low overall capitals, which makes it impossible for them to climb upwards on either the economic or the cultural ladder. What perhaps introduces an extra nuance to this version of the taste of necessity argument is that in the functionality discourse, there is a fervent belief that saving money does not only mean choosing the only option available; it can also be equated to a resourceful and ingenious way of engaging in cultural participation. In general, the functionality discourse makes it clear that cultural participation can occur even at the recycling bin or by going to sales.

OPENNESS AND TOLERANCE

A recurring theme in the functionality discourse includes expressions of openness and tolerance. Instead of discussing them at a more general level, the interviewees usually presented them as practical corollaries of their own practices: whatever cultural participation worked for them was considered good and valuable and was defended as such. This attitude went hand in hand with an idea of a somewhat superficial openness and tolerance: whatever is considered 'my thing' is OK, whereas someone else has 'their thing', which I cannot object to. In the interviews, this sometimes led to denials of any kind of negative distinctions in relation to other peoples' cultural practices: people were keen to say that they unpleasant culture did not exist simply because they never came across any. Like the retired hairdresser Julia put it when asked about what she considered unpleasant reading: 'In my life, there is nothing repulsive. You have to have a positive attitude'.

The concept of 'my thing' and of respecting the others' cultural practices was recurrent throughout the data. One could perhaps see this as a Finnish version of the Law of Jante, made famous by the Danish-Norwegian author Aksel Sandemose in his 1933 satirical novel *A Fugitive Crosses His Tracks*, in which he presents ten rules or codes of conduct of the fictitious Danish village of Jante, often summarised as 'You should not think you are anyone special, or better than us'. The Law of Jante is often seen as the backbone of Nordic egalitarianism: society is put ahead of the individual, and self-praise is criticised. In this context, portraying unfamiliar and unpleasant cultural products simply as 'not my thing' can be seen as a way of conveniently avoiding boundary-drawing and putting perceived others ahead of oneself:

> Anniina: Yeah, so war books are not kind of my thing, I can't stand it. Also, I don't watch war movies because they are not my thing in that way, but if there is history in it, if it's not only war, then I'm interested.
> RH: OK. Regarding newspapers and magazines, is there anything revolting that you would not read?
> Anniina: No, I read so little that whatever I read, I'm interested in it. It could be something like *Kauneus & Terveys* and *Fit* and *SPORT* [fitness magazines]. I don't really know, I read too few magazines that if I sit somewhere waiting, I might maybe read something. It's not kind of my thing [laughs].
> RH: And about music, what's close to your heart?
> Anniina: Oh damn… I am, like, kind of anything goes, it depends so much on my state of mind. The only thing that is not quite my thing is this real death-thrash-metal, I cannot stand that growling.
> (Anniina, 39, unemployed salesperson)

> RH (showing the art elicitation photos): What about number five?
> Maarit: I like its colours but… It's nice. This… I am not sure. That one might make it to my wall, but I'm not sure. That angularity is somehow not quite my thing. It has something weirdly dark. But something mysterious too, in a nice way.
> (Maarit, 37, student)

> RH: You like museums?
> Melissa: Well no.
> RH: What's the thing about them?
> Melissa: I don't know, they just somehow are not my thing.
> (Melissa, NA, disability pensioner)

The idea of 'my thing' being as valuable as anyone else's in the field of cultural participation comes together with a potential openness to and tolerance of new things—which, again, is well documented in the scholarly literature in relation to resource-rich rather than resource-poor societal groups (Lindblom 2022; Peterson and Kern 1996). The particularity or the functionality discourse lies in highlighting that one is not bothered by certain unpleasant cultural practices:

Tuomo (speaking about repulsive music): Well, I don't know, there is a button on TV for getting rid of it. It does not bother me in that way, even though I would not listen to it.
(Tuomo, 77, retired engineer)

RH: Do you go to classical music concerts?
Joni: In high school I think I once attended, it was part of a course that you would have to listen to a concert and write a review.
RH: Oh. Did you like it?
Joni: Well, it was OK. As a rare experience it was just fine.
(Joni, 35, disability pensioner)

Unlike in the affirmation discourse discussed in Chap. 5, which emphasised learning and acquiring tastes, the functionality discourse highlights more the potentiality of *tolerating* new things. For instance, when 33-year-old unemployed salesperson Sara speaks about opera and classical music concerts (which she never attends), she makes a point about the fact that she *could go*, if the circumstances were right, and even if it was not 'her thing'. 'I might go if I got a ticket, I'm usually a kind of person that goes if someone gives me a free ticket and if it fits me, but well, it's not as I'm too interested (…) it's not terribly much my thing, but of course I could be surprised. So I am kind of open about these things'. Sara repeats the same idea more in depth when talking about restaurants:

Probably it's because of all those different spices that I never go to these Nepalese places. It's not maybe my thing, but I have not gone too much, I have not given them too much of an opportunity. If a friend would ask me to eat there, I would go and try to find something in the menu. Another thing that I have never eaten too much, in fact I have never eaten it in a restaurant, is sushi. (…) In some shop some cook made tasters and I've tried it and it's fine, but I've never been to the restaurant having sushi, that's the thing. But I would give it a chance (…) Somehow, this raw fish and rice and that kind of thing does not attract me, but I would give it a chance. So, I am pretty open-minded about those things.
(Sara, 33, unemployed salesperson)

Some interviewees make it even clearer that complicated or exotic cultural practices are, rather than being directly contested, simply disregarded because they are not even seen as possible for the 'likes of me'. Like Emma, the 34-year-old unemployed graduate of a commercial institute, puts it when asked whether there are any restaurants that she would not like:

> Emma: Perhaps these Chinese places and that kind of stuff, it's not my style of food. (…) I'm maybe not used to eating them. Although yes, I could eat them.
> RH: Does it have to do with the spices, or?
> Emma: Maybe yes. I've never thought why, I just have an image that they don't have my type of food.

Tolerance Even When There Is a Lack of Resources: Case Max

I meet Max in a free meeting room at the central library of Helsinki. He apologises for being late; he took a train from the distant suburb where he lives and got mixed up with the public transport zone system, new at the time of the interview.

Max is 39 years old. Since finishing compulsory education, he has completed two different degrees in vocational school—first he became a computer mechanic and, then, a car mechanic. He has worked in different fields, sometimes in several jobs simultaneously: as a car salesperson, as an IT support person and a DJ and karaoke host, as well as working in his family's service business. At the time of the interview, he has been unemployed for some years but is actively looking for a job.

Losing his job has meant a total paradigm change in Max's previously very busy life ('at least what I myself have noticed as a big change is that when you're unemployed you have free time; you have to invent things to do, previously you would not have to, the agenda would be filled anyway'). Max's hobbies have all undergone changes because of the lack of money related to being unemployed: instead of going to the gym, he trains at home ('that has again to do with the expenses, it would swallow too large a share of my monthly budget'), and instead of belonging to many associations related to vehicles and rare plants, he now has to cultivate his garden on his own ('These activities have pretty much come to a halt with this unemployment, as both would require quite a lot of moving around and taking care of things. So, again the problem is the budget, and how to move around and visit events around Finland and that kind of thing').

(*continued*)

(continued)

Even with this apparent exclusion factor, Max exhibits some patterns of everyday participation: he likes cooking and mentions that many friends often visit him bringing a plastic bag of ingredients with them, with the idea that Max will cook for everyone. He speaks at length about the importance of avoiding convenience food and finding fresh and high-quality ingredients and has tried to avoid meat for some years now. He loves going to discos (while lamenting that the nineties rave culture has faded away) and on spontaneous road trips.

Although many highbrow-oriented events initially interest Max, he finds it a distant idea to go to, for instance, a classical music concert or the theatre ('maybe it's also that in my circle of friends, there's not that kind of people'). The interesting thing about Max is actually his tolerant attitude towards highbrow culture: even though he never participates in it, he labels his view as 'neutral': 'I do not find it repulsive, but, those are things that I never cross paths with in my everyday life, so I just don't pay attention to them'. This same tolerance is present when thinking about restaurants that he would not like to eat in: 'I cannot think of any. Nothing occurs to me. I am kind of quite open-minded about them, probably everywhere there is at least something good and interesting that you can learn from'.

Max is a good example of the increasing importance of the ideals of cultural openness and tolerance in general (Peterson 2005). His case highlights well Ollivier's argument (2008) that automatically associating openness with privileged groups and closure with underprivileged groups is erroneous; tolerance can be such a salient part of the ethos of especially younger groups that it is necessarily not *only* part of the repertoires of privileged groups (cf. Lindblom 2022).

We have seen that an emphasis on openness and tolerance is a central part of the functionality discourse. However, it should be pointed out that actual cultural participation repertoires represented in the functionality discourse remain limited: although highbrow-oriented cultural participation such as theatre or classical music concerts is initially depicted in a positive and open-minded light—for instance, eating exotic food is considered a possibility—many times, such activities are mentally located far away from everyday life to the point of being invisible.

MODESTY

In the interview guidelines, the last question concerned 'the day of my dreams'. The question was originally intended to contrast the content that I expected to get from the rest of the interviews—the idea was that, with potentially somewhat limited cultural participation or practices being very much restrained by structural factors or a lack of resources, the interviewees would at least have the chance to describe their *potential* or *desired* cultural participation—the things that they would do if there were no restraints.

Although I expected to listen to dreams that would, at least in some way, be related to higher resources, I was surprised to find that most people daydreamed of extremely moderate, economically and culturally modest activities—things that probably already formed a part of the interviewees' realities. For instance, the 77-year-old retired Tuomo dreamed of an outdoor excursion, 'campfire coffee in an open-air tent, that kind of thing'. Emma, a 34-year-old unemployed graduate of a commercial institute, said that she would like to go to the hairdresser's and have a facial treatment. Jarmo, 67, a pensioner from the north of Finland like Tuomo, dreamed about visiting Helsinki once in his lifetime with an airplane. The interviewees in Focus Group 7 with three regulars of a bar in a small town said that they would actually like to spend the day of their dreams in the very same bar:

> Raisa: I don't know whether I would really wish for that, but yes, if I had the whole day free (…) and I would not have to go to work or anything like that, I would surely spend that whole day here.

These modest dreams, of course, are a stellar example of what Bourdieu means by his idea of a 'sense of one's place', an unconscious approval of existing hierarchies in which 'the social order is progressively inscribed in people's minds (…) objective limits become a sense of limits, a practical anticipation of objective limits acquired by experience of objective limits, a "sense of one's place" which leads one to exclude oneself from the goods, persons, places and so forth from which one is excluded' (Bourdieu 1984/1979, 471). Milla and Jarkko, the young couple interviewed in Focus Group 4, state that their absolute dream would be to go to IKEA. Instead of involving pure pleasure, the dream has practical underpinnings:

RH: So what would you buy from IKEA if you could make it there?
Milla: Well probably some clever storage racks for those cupboards, cause now you feel the cutlery swings around when you open the drawer, it doesn't stay in place. And then for the utility room, I would get some sort of smarter laundry sorting system or a more functional solution. And other than that, probably all kinds of useless decorating stuff from scented candles to artificial flowers [laughs]. Some curtains and rugs that I would probably never use, but at least I would have them.

In the above quotation, Milla's tone has slight hints of boundary-drawing: smart and functional storage racks and laundry sorting systems are good, but 'useless decorating stuff' is something to laugh about. In the functionality discourse, there is, in general, a broad consensus about modest yet well-working cultural practices being valuable and 'useless' unpractical cultural practices unvaluable, even ridiculous. This seems to be another way of using one's modesty as a means of drawing upward boundaries. In the interviews, homes and living spaces were typical examples of exhibiting these kinds of attitudes. Echoing Southerton's findings on how locally based communities share and confirm the tastes of people 'round here', creating class-based distinctions between functional versus individualistic kitchens (Southerton 2001), there were strong statements in the interviews about the superiority of functional choices—always related to small critical upwards boundaries, as evidenced by the interviewees' talk on their homes:

Well, it's a detached house, it does not have to be any kind of luxury standard, it's not as if I would like to live in luxury, that's what we have.
(Tuomo, 77, retired engineer)

Well, it's definitely not a house from interior design magazines (…) it has a bit of everything, but it's a cosy-looking home.
(Laura, 28, bus driver)

(My childhood home) was extremely poor, there was nothing except for that basic furniture… but otherwise it was OK. There were no paintings, no nothing, it had the basic furniture from those days.
(Silja, 64, retired mixed manual worker)

From cultural practices often described as 'normal', there is in fact not a long way to drawing boundaries against things considered 'too fancy':

Basic home food is what I (like), I'm not (interested) in that kind of terribly fine fancy portions or special things, rather basic home food, that's maybe more my thing.
(Anniina, 39, unemployed salesperson)

Usually, I seek to buy kind of durable (furniture) and look after them; I don't usually just buy furniture kind of like, 'I fancy decorating my house so I'll go to burn money in Vepsäläinen [quality design furniture shop]'– no way.
(Sami, 37, cook)

Eero, a 30-year-old kiosk worker with a rather hostile attitude to most highbrow-oriented cultural practices, tells me what he considers to be a sad story of having to move houses, when he was a child, to a 'fancier' part of town: what he had perceived as a relaxed life of running in the yard and shouting to other neighbours through the balconies was now replaced by 'rigid' new neighbours: 'They were this (…) high living standard kind of people, kind of like "our life is better than yours"'. When Eero later talks about how he would like to live in the future, his dreams involve highly similar tones to what we have encountered earlier:

I would like to make it kind of in a way that it resembles me, nothing ostentatious, rather something that fits a normal Joe Public, something that everyone can afford.

Modesty, as we have seen, is an essential part of the functionality discourse. At first glance, this may seem like a practical example of Bourdieu's 'sense of one's place' (1984/1979, 417)—interviewees were keen to demonstrate their unpretentiousness and, to a certain degree, voluntary abstention from pursuing expensive or luxurious cultural practices. However, when scrutinised more closely, the emphasis on modesty revealed the symbolic boundaries present in the functionality discourse: here, the interviewees drew mostly aesthetical boundaries upwards, representing 'unnecessary' or impractical cultural participation and items, such as fine dining and luxury homes, which were presented under the guise of it not being 'my thing'. It could perhaps also be speculated that in the functionality discourse, modesty works as a strategy of showing the interviewees' cultural deference towards the interviewer (see Jarness and Flemmen 2019): a way of securing their dignity and self-worth by emphasising that their cultural practices do match their class position.

CONCLUSION: A LACK OF BOUNDARIES?

Within the functionality discourse, there is mainly popular and everyday participation. What distinguishes cultural participation in this discourse from that of the other two discourses is the emphasis on practical usefulness in a broad sense: reading or listening to music is practised for the relax they offer, sports is a way of staying fit and showing worthiness, and watching television offers a welcome distraction from the difficulties of daily life or hard and tiring work. Cultural participation thus entails a strongly instrumental motivation—it is an area of personal and well-deserved 'feelgood'.

We have seen that the functionality discourse is marked, first of all, by a strong link between cultural participation and the many structuring factors of life. Cultural participation is presented as something entertaining and amusing that can ease or smooth out everyday hardships by pushing them aside for a while. At the same time, cultural participation is rarely conceived of as something through which it would be possible to create lifestyle distinctions. In this sense, my Finnish interviewees resemble the UK working classes in the sense that their cultural practices involved an 'orientation towards goods, fun and entertainment' (Bennett et al. 2009, 205). At the same time, the interviewees strongly emphasised the practicality or rationality of their cultural practices and even framed a certain lack of resources (such as the lack of money) as possible avenues for expressing ingenuity and, eventually, self-worth.

The functionality discourse was also traversed by a stress on openness. Many interviewees cherished, at least superficially, the idea that 'anything goes' or that cultural practices are—or are not—'one's thing'. It could be interpreted, though, that this apparent openness and tolerance are somewhat superficial. Many interviewees said that they were 'open to everything' but, in fact, had limited preferences—resembling here Ollivier's 'indifferent openness' (Ollivier 2008). This superficiality became even more apparent when symbolic boundaries entered the game: in the functionality discourse, there is an emphasis on modesty and a certain acceptance of one's low position in the social hierarchy, but the discourse hides the boundaries drawn upwards. The boundaries are mostly aesthetical and directed upwards towards impractical, non-functional cultural participation and items (fine dining, luxury homes, etc. portrayed as 'not my thing'). This is a clear difference from the affirmation discourse, which

---

only drew downward aesthetical boundaries. In other words, in the functionality discourse, there are delicate traces of anti-elitism. Here, cultural participation played a mainly practical role, and the interviewees did not link it with the possibility of accumulating cultural capital, unlike in the affirmation discourse—they took cultural participation with a certain laxness and indifference. This resembles the finding of Vassenden and Jonvik (2019), whereby interviewees with a low position in the social hierarchy showed 'little deference to the tastes and culture of the more educated' and did not 'express feelings of subordination, of being looked down on for their tastes or lack of education' (Vassenden and Jonvik 2019, 38). In this sense, the indifferent and at the same time self-assured attitude towards cultural participation that characterises the functionality discourse could perfectly be a version of egalitarianism.

References

Bauman Z (1991) *Modernity and ambivalence*. Cambridge: Polity Press.
Bennett T, Savage M, Silva E, Warde A, Gayo-Cal M and Wright D (2009) *Culture, Class, Distinction*. London: Routledge.
Blasius J and Friedrichs J (2008) Lifestyles in distressed neighborhoods: A test of Bourdieu's "taste of necessity" hypothesis. *Poetics* 36(1): 24–44.
Bourdieu P (1984/1979) *Distinction. A Social Critique of the Judgment of Taste*. London: Routledge & Kegan Paul.
Featherstone M (1991) *Consumer culture and postmodernism*. London: Sage.
Jarness V and Flemmen M (2019) A struggle on two fronts: Boundary drawing in the lower region of the social space and the symbolic market for "down-to-earthness". *British Journal of Sociology* 70: 166–189.
Kahma N (2012) Sport and social class: The case of Finland. *International Review for the Sociology of Sport* 47(1), 113–130.
Levine LW (1988) *Highbrow/Lowbrow: The Emergence of Cultural Hierarchy in America*. Cambridge, MA: Harvard University Press.
Lindblom T (2022) Growing openness or creeping intolerance? Cultural taste orientations and tolerant social attitudes in Finland, 2007–2018. *Poetics*. Available at: https://doi.org/10.1016/j.poetic.2022.101663. (Accessed 21 August 2022).
Miles A and Sullivan A (2012) Understanding participation in culture and sport: Mixing methods, reordering knowledges. *Cultural Trends* 21(4): 311–324.
Ollivier M (2008) Modes of openness to cultural diversity. Humanist, populist, practical, and indifferent. *Poetics* 36 (2–3): 120–147.
Peterson RA (2005) Problems in comparative research: the example of omnivorousness. *Poetics* 33(5–6): 257–282.

Peterson RA and Kern R (1996) Changing Highbrow Taste: From Snob to Omnivore. *American Sociological Review* 61(5): 900–907.

Sandemose A (1933/1936). *A Fugitive Crosses his Tracks.* New York: Alfred A. Knopp.

Skeggs B and Loveday V (2012) Struggles for Value: Value Practices, Injustice, Judgment, Affect and the Idea of Class. *The British Journal of Sociology* 63(3): 472–490.

Southerton D (2001) Consuming Kitchens: Taste, context and identity formation. *Journal of Consumer Culture* 1(2): 179–203.

Vassenden A and Jonvik M (2019) Cultural Capital as a Hidden Asset: Culture, Egalitarianism and Inter-Class Social Encounters in Stavanger, Norway. *Cultural Sociology* 13(1): 37–56.

CHAPTER 7

Resistance

Abstract This chapter focuses on the resistance discourse which is inclined towards popular and everyday cultural participation. The discourse is based on an opposition to the norm of highbrow-oriented cultural participation. Most methodological challenges of the interviews are especially related to this discourse. The boundaries drawn in the resistance discourse are basically all directed upwards. They are either aesthetical (directed against highbrow-oriented cultural practices) or moral (directed against people considered snobbish). There is strong awareness of exploitation in the resistance discourse. People close to the resistance discourse are aware of their low status, but they call for being treated as equals. In the resistance discourse, clearly situated the furthest away from normative cultural participation, there is a desire for egalitarianism.

Keywords Resistance discourse • Defiance • Counter-talk • Upward symbolic boundaries • Egalitarianism

Prologue

I meet Marko at the restaurant of the practically only hotel in his small home village. Marko is 47 years old, has no formal education and works as a farmer on his own farm. His work is highly seasonal—I am interviewing

© The Author(s) 2022, corrected publication 2023   111
R. Heikkilä, *Understanding Cultural Non-Participation in an Egalitarian Context*, Palgrave Studies in Cultural Participation,
https://doi.org/10.1007/978-3-031-18865-7_7

him in wintertime when he has lots of free time. He has a wife and one teenage child.

Marko is one of the most curious interviewees of the entire sample: he is verbally highly talented and witty and converts the interview situation into an opportunity to crack jokes, to tell shocking details about his life and even to make fun at the expense of the 'formal' interview situation. For instance, he states that his favourite food is 'anything that makes me fart', constantly mentions watching pornography and making illegal moonshine and brags about his boisterous drinking habits. He tells stories of how he sometimes attends concerts just for the joy of getting drunk or how he once had rolled down the incredibly long stairs of the hotel in which the interview is held ('It was just like in a movie... I shot the rapids but they were dry, like they say'). He knows the personnel of the hotel and shouts something to them from time to time.

Marko is opposed to highbrow culture tooth and nail and mocks it throughout the interview. Although he might sometimes read books on military issues or hunting, he rarely touches anything else. He explains his hate in graphic detail: 'Some sort of unnecessary dragged-out biography with 1600 pages will certainly remain unfinished – if I ever manage to even start. I don't have the energy to sit absorbed in that. (...) Blah blah blah, fiddle-faddle, the same drag from cover to cover. No. Who could ever examine all that. If you don't have a migraine before you start, you will certainly have it afterwards'. Of the local arts and crafts museum, he says: 'I have any number of that same rubbish at home. There is no point to go to marvel them at the museum'.

Marko's cultural practices mostly revolve around popular cultural participation. He has gone to the circus with his child ('Even though I'm pretty much a clown myself, so it was not so much needed'). He watches TV, mostly reality shows and quizzes ('Do you want to be a millionaire... Well, of course I do. I've tried out poverty, and this is nothing to shout about, so I could be a millionaire for a change'). In movies, he likes action, especially Arnold Schwarzenegger. He says he is 'pretty omnivorous' regarding music: he listens to classical musical sometimes, but more commonly to pop, rock, heavy music and speed metal. His all-time favourite band is Rammstein, which he has even seen live ('Went to see them with a friend just to be able to get really drunk – we did succeed').

Marko is also highly active in things that are perfect examples of everyday participation. His main hobby is fixing written-off cars and finding spare parts through his networks. He also attends kettlebell classes and goes to the gym; belongs to a vintage car association, a Volkswagen fans' association and a hunting association; and has often acted as treasurer or secretary. He picks berries and mushrooms, and when the season starts, he goes elk hunting. He uses internet daily ('I do watch also things that are not pornography') and belongs to many WhatsApp groups of different vehicle associations. He travels abroad for vacations from time to time ('Canary Islands, pretty much. This traditional favourite destination of Finns. You go to the Canary Islands and get smashed').

Marko draws many upward moral boundaries; for instance, he is annoyed by an early #MeToo case in Finland, in which film director Aku Louhimies was accused by female actresses of using questionable methods in his work ('You should let the man be in peace, he has asked for forgiveness'). He appreciates unpretentiousness and dislikes people who get upset too easily ('What does it matter if you sometimes take the piss out of somebody? That will just refresh them. (...) People whine about everything these days').

A DIFFERENT 'EVERYDAY PARTICIPATION'

Marko is an excellent example of the resistance discourse: he maintains a hostile attitude towards highbrow-oriented cultural practices, but at the same time, he has lots of both popular and everyday participation. In other words, when observed superficially, the resistance discourse has similar cultural participation patterns as the functionality discourse—and even the affirmation discourse, even if the affirmation discourse also includes highbrow-oriented cultural participation. What distinguishes the resistance discourse from the two other discourses is the heavily defiant and critical tone, which is sometimes even mocking and rebellious, as clearly revealed by Marko's interview. While traditional highbrow-oriented cultural participation is seen as something positive and desirable for the affirmation discourse and a possible or tolerable option—at most, 'not my thing'—in the functionality discourse, for the resistance discourse, anything close to highbrow culture is seen as directly repellent.

Therefore, it is not surprising to find this kind of hostility towards established cultural practices among the lower classes. Bourdieu famously considered the lower classes to be passive and willing to accept the 'taste of necessity'. He argued that as the lower classes had few economic resources, their practically oriented cultural practices could be interpreted as a surrender to the surrounding conditions, which the lower classes themselves explained as supposedly their own choice (Bourdieu 1984/1979, 380). This view of a submissive lower class has been heavily criticised later: scholars of many different contexts have shown that, on the contrary, there are feelings of resentment and anger among the lower classes (Hochschild 2016; Lamont 2018). Unlike the somewhat docile image painted by Bourdieu, subsequent scholars have argued that the lower classes are aware of being exploited (De Keere 2020; Savage et al. 2015), perceiving themselves as judged and their cultural practices as devalued (Skeggs and Loveday 2012). The most precarious groups often perceive living under a stigma (Savage et al. 2015) which is further corroborated through discriminatory labels, such as 'chav' (Jones 2016) or 'underclass' (Tyler 2013).

A considerable difference from the other discourses is that in the resistance discourse, there seems to be no inherent idea about that cultural participation—or even leisure activities—should be particularly enjoyable, a vehicle for learning new things or a means of relaxing, as in the affirmation and functionality discourses. Many interviewees shunned the idea of 'free time' altogether and dedicated it to working in the house, walking the dog or minding the children. For instance, Marketta, a 69-year-old pensioner who worked as a guard and was a single mother, becomes offended when asked about hobbies which she considers a luxury out of her reach: 'Work, work, and the brats, that's all I had'. Many other accounts show that cultural participation, although it exists, is not necessarily linked to personal enjoyment or fulfilment:

> RH: What do you do if you have a moment before you go to sleep yourself?
> Olli: Well, I probably browse my phone, for a couple of days I've been playing web poker just for fun, and I noticed already yesterday night that, well, this is starting to get really boring, so…
> RH: Is it captivating?
> Olli: It's not captivating at all. Maybe, if the stakes were thousands of euros instead of just a couple of euros, that could bring on some excitement, but now it's not interesting at all.
> (Olli, 41, machine operator)

> RH: How much do you use the internet?
> Emma: Well at this moment I don't have a computer, my only internet access is through the phone.
> RH: OK. And do you use it daily?

> Emma: Well, yes, there is nothing else to do, so I scroll Facebook up and down [laughs].
> RH: Anything else that you do at home, is there anything, crosswords or handwork...?
> Emma: Not nowadays, I just watch the telly and try to entertain myself in some way. But when I have more energy, I do a hell of a lot of handicrafts.
> (Emma, 34, unemployed)

In the resistance discourse, in addition to hostility, there is also considerable cultural activity. Thus, it would be wrong to say that the resistance discourse is devoid of participation; rather, participation falls outside of the categories typically considered in different surveys. Side by side with the resistance discourse there are practices such as hunting, berry-picking, building computers out of spare parts, geocaching, collecting old coins and so on, many of which are stellar examples of items that rarely make it onto different surveys measuring cultural participation (Flemmen et al. 2018; Savage et al. 2015).

> In the summer I like to go running. Right now there's not really that possibility yet. But mainly I like to be on my own. (...) I fix computers, I build computers for my friends (...) or displays for phones. That kind of handiwork has been a counterbalance for the typical thing (...) I speak to people so much that I can't do so much handiwork. So it's a nice counterbalance for that.
> (Eero, 30, kiosk worker)

> Lasse: Actually there are not many things I like... well, my hobby is to follow football through the website of Veikkaus...
> RH: Do you bet money yourself?
> Lasse: Yeah, always a couple of euros a day. Well, in the long run, I am, of course, losing money, but lately, it's been plus or minus zero. That's it. I also surf a little bit on social media and watch different kinds of videos.
> (Lasse, 56, unemployed)

Lack of Legitimate Cultural Practices Does Not Equal to Passivity:
Case Olli

I meet Olli at the same shopping mall café that I used earlier for meeting Olli's wife, Minna (see Chap. 5). Minna has been keen to find me more interviewees and has persuaded her husband, a 41-year-old machine operator in a factory, to be interviewed. This is probably why Olli initially has a positive attitude: he asks me in advance whether he needs to take something with him to the interview, and his considered responses reveal that he has clearly thought about the interview topics in advance. Olli speaks openly about his many worries connected to the structural factors of life: the fact that he might become fired due to outsourcing plans in the factory in which he works and the family's current difficulties with selling a flat.

Olli's cultural practices are those of a stereotypical working-class male. He engages in practically no highbrow-oriented participation. He never reads anything—in fact he does not remember ever having read a book, and he never reads any newspapers or magazines, except for a commercial leaflet of a retail store selling tools ('something like a Biltema catalogue could be something that I might browse a little bit'). He listens to the Hitmix radio channel and sometimes to heavy metal and considers himself, music-wise, 'pretty much an omnivore, with the exception of opera, jazz and classical music'. He does not recognise any of the paintings shown to him, but he likes them and connects them to memories ('this picture of the crow reminds me of last summer with my own son, when he chased crows out of the tree, that's what makes me feel good about the painting'). Although Olli never goes to classical music concerts, he has gone to the ballet once because his wife insisted—but like we know from Minna's account, they felt out of place ('we were not ourselves at all... I think I even fell asleep a bit').

However, Olli engages in many other activities and is highly active in practices that fall both under popular and everyday participation. He is a fervent enthusiast of shooting: in his family, there is a long tradition of hunting, and lately Olli has joined a shooting club. He speaks at length about the many bureaucratic issues surrounding gun permits. He likes to go out to eat at American and Mexican

(continued)

(continued)

chain restaurants ('basic places, nothing too fine') and remembers with horror some of the times he ended up at a restaurant that he considered too fancy ('the waiters were really surprised and the food was some kind of greasy duck tenderloin, my god, we just hid it, it was too fine for us'). Olli is also a devoted father who spends lots of time with his toddler child and wishes to take him to a combat sports activity later on ('in order to take care of himself and his self-esteem') and asks me, after the interview, about my ideas and best tips regarding potty training.

Olli is a good example of the fact that a striking lack of highbrow-oriented cultural participation does not mean a lack of activity in general (see Heikkilä 2021). In fact, profiles such as Olli's are easily labelled with 'morally derogative terms' (Flemmen et al. 2018, 23) simply because their activities do not match with what is asked in most quantitative surveys measuring cultural participation.

Savage et al. (2015) argue that there is a strong division between, on the one hand, active participation in the 'public world' and, on the other hand, an aversion or dislike of many cultural practices. Moreover, they go on to argue that an active orientation is 'more socially approved of – more legitimate' (Savage et al. 2015, 105). This link to social approval is probably the key to understanding properly the resistance discourse. This discourse shuns highbrow-oriented, publicly recognised cultural practices while embracing at least some items from the fields of popular and everyday culture—yet with undertones of resentment and anger towards potentially judgemental upper classes (Skeggs and Loveday 2012). The idea of everyday participation, a possible compensation for 'lacking' cultural engagement, as a 'considerable informal involvement in kin-based and local circles, and in home-based activities' (Bennett et al. 2009, 64) or as a signal of social capital and social networks (Miles and Gibson 2016) does not fully capture this.

AN UNKNOWN TERRITORY

In the affirmation and functionality discourses, there seems to be a shared understanding of the value of highbrow-oriented cultural participation—in short, it is commonly recognised and legitimised (Bourdieu 1984/1979) as something connected to public culture and possible cultural capital. In the resistance discourse, there is nothing of this. Highbrow-oriented culture represents an unfamiliar territory, a no-comfort zone and a sphere of standards that the interviewees felt they were unable to meet.

A typical milieu of discomfort is the educational system—something we know plays an important role in legitimising highbrow culture and making highbrow-oriented cultural practices seem the 'natural' skills of middle and upper class children, who have actually inherited these skills from home and are thus able to pursue different forms of capital (Bourdieu 1986; Bourdieu and Darbel 1991; Bourdieu and Passeron 1979). School has traditionally been a place in which the working classes have had to fight harder than the middle classes for educational success (Loveday 2015; Willis 1977/2017). A central part of the resistance discourse is the recollection of school as a forced formality, an institution that tried to impose upon the interviewees the cultural practices they were naturally opposed to. The retired Jarmo, 67, that worked as a car painter, among other jobs, remembers the following words of his schoolteacher: 'You won't pass school just by skating and singing'. For many interviewees, reading and writing sadly remain especially traumatic experiences that teachers rubbed in their faces. A member of Focus Group 8 of a pensioners' association in a small city shares the following memory: 'If you would write something wrongly, the teacher would ask you to read it out loud and (...) how is it possible to express yourself like this, they would kind of point you out and make a jibe at you. That's the typical power the teacher has'. The feeling of having been forced to read touches upon also younger interviewees:

> How I hated as a kid when in school when you were forced to read something! It has probably remained from there, this feeling that you don't like to read books.
> (Emma, 34, unemployed)

> I really don't like to read at all. When they forced me to read some books in primary school, I did not like them at all, and then it came to nothing. Well, sometimes, I do read something, horror books or something like that.
> (Focus Group 1, Sonja, 18, student at a vocational school)

A related phenomenon is that the resistance discourse often conceives of highbrow-oriented cultural practices as ridiculous, something to be openly laughed at. In the sociology of culture, it is well documented that laughing off questions in formal interviews is a way of distancing oneself from the interview situation and showing awareness of possible top-down stereotyping (Heikkilä and Katainen 2021; Savage et al. 2015). In the same vein, humour in itself is strongly linked to symbolic boundary-drawing and to moral judgements (Friedman and Kuipers 2013; Kuipers 2015)—laughing about something is an effective vehicle for class distinctions. Typical examples included the many quasi-classical comments made about the ridiculous features of highbrow-oriented culture:

> Anniina (speaking about opera): As an experience I believe it would be absolutely wonderful... If they would not scream and if it had more men, why not! (laughter)
> RH: OK, so you would give it a chance.
> Anniina: Yes, I would bear it for a little while (laughter)
> (Anniina, 39, unemployed)

> RH: OK. What about art exhibitions?
> Mimosa: Could not interest me less.
> RH: Can you tell what it is that does not interest you?
> Mimosa: I think it's silly to stare at some vases or paintings that have a line in the middle or two spots or... Nope.
> (Mimosa, 37, cleaner)

> Lukas (speaking about why he does not attend museums): Well, in Finland what prevents me is that museums are so anaemic (laughter). If you go to the National Gallery and look at a 'modern Finn', you will see people in shell suits and a box of Weetabix in some corner, and you're like, 'I can't believe this is true' (laughter). You can walk through the whole thing in ten minutes. And, on top of everything, you are expected to pay for it.
> (Lukas, 41, unemployed)

Another layer of this discomfort involves mocking the entire topic of the interview—that is, cultural participation and practices more widely. It is well known from previous research that culture can be a touchy subject (Heikkilä and Katainen 2021), and this is why this research intended to capture broadly leisure instead of only 'culture' following the model of Ollivier (2008). Still, the resistance discourse emphasised its open dislike of cultural practices considered simply stupid or 'too fine for us', in addition to being disgusting and intolerable.

This open dislike was most typically expressed as a feeling of having troubles understanding what (highbrow-oriented) culture is about or having been 'left behind' of it, which usually went in tandem with a feeling of being left behind in society more generally. For instance, Lasse, a 56-year-old unemployed man with a long history of performing different manual jobs with their many structural problems throughout the years from recession-related layoffs to organisational changes ('organisation renewals and that kind of stuff, and automatisation'), describes having gone through so much frustration in his own life that he has lost sympathy for others—a rather typical example of the prototypical working-class male who is in a vicious circle of downward mobility, deprivation and a perceived loss of power (Gest 2016). This pattern is perhaps particularly evident in his media use: he has stopped reading Finland's by far largest quality newspaper, *Helsingin Sanomat*, and *Kansan Uutiset* (*People's News*, the Left Alliance's official Finnish-language weekly newspaper). This is how Lasse explains it:

> There started to be things that they emphasise a lot that did not speak to me anymore, well, like feminism and this kind of stuff. I don't have the energy to be sympathetic towards everybody. I have had some issues in my own life, lots of work with it, I don't have energy for that kind of stuff anymore.

Finally, the resistance discourse includes a common understanding of the fact that normative highbrow-oriented cultural participation is simply too difficult to be properly understood. For instance, Sonja, an 18-year-old vocational school student from a city in the north of Finland, aptly summarises that she does not go to art exhibitions: 'I don't understand anything about art [laughs] it sure looks fine, but deeper down, I know nothing about it'. Olli, the 41-year-old machine operator, speaks about his many embarrassing moments in restaurants when he has not known how to act: 'We did not know the purpose of all that cutlery, so we looked at other tables to see in which order you have to use them'. The farmer Marko, whom we already know from the prologue of this chapter, gives a telling reason for why he dislikes many newspapers and magazines, among them the investigative journalism magazine *Suomen Kuvalehti* (lit. *Finland's Picture Magazine*, a classical magazine founded in 1873 focusing on national and international politics and culture from a centre-right stance) whose readership is linked to high education and highbrow-oriented cultural practices (Purhonen et al. 2014): 'Well for instance

Suomen Kuvalehti (…) most of it is so tedious and impenetrable and complicated'.

These accounts reflect well Bourdieu's idea that access to arts or high culture can never refer only to physical accessibility; rather, access to arts is intrinsically linked to the capacity of deciphering and finally understanding them (Bourdieu 1993). Cultural capital can be seen here as a form of information, as an internalised code, that helps people (or not) to understand cultural items. Bourdieu holds that without knowledge and recognition, cultural items do not even exist in a value system: '(W)orks of arts exist as symbolic objects only if they are known and recognized, that is, socially instituted as works of art and received by spectators capable of knowing and recognizing them as such' (Bourdieu 1993, 37). It has become clear that within the resistance discourse, there is not (enough) of this knowledge and recognition, and consequently normative highbrow-oriented cultural participation feels alienating and boring, even humiliating. However, this bold and straightforward attitude associated with this discourse is highly different from Bourdieu's image of the passive lower classes who simply accept their 'taste of necessity'. In the following sub-chapters, we will investigate more deeply the kinds of symbolic boundaries drawn in the resistance discourse.

HOSTILITY: AESTHETICAL UPWARD BOUNDARIES

We have seen that the affirmation discourse mostly draws downward boundaries, both aesthetical (against lowbrow cultural practices) and moral (against laziness and not doing anything). The functionality discourse draws only upward boundaries which were exclusively aesthetical (against impractical and non-functional cultural practices—always presented under the tolerant umbrella of 'not my thing'). Meanwhile, the resistance discourse draws only upward boundaries (like the functionality discourse), both aesthetical and moral ones. The aesthetical upward boundaries mainly involve highbrow-oriented cultural practices (opera, ballet, classical music, museums and so on), presented as ridiculous, disgusting or directly intolerable. This, of course, is unsurprising in the light of the existing literature, most famously Bourdieu's idea of aesthetic intolerance as a violent force: 'Aversion to different life-styles is perhaps one of the strongest barriers between the classes' (Bourdieu 1984/1979, 56). In the resistance discourse, there is clearly a strong aversion against high culture, which most commonly manifests itself in relation to the most obvious items of highbrow-oriented culture: ballet, opera, high art and so on. Here, the art photo elicitation part of the interviews was very fruitful, with the findings supporting the argument of Vassenden and Jonvik (2021) according to which different cultural areas bring out highly different interview speech.

Although all art photos were perhaps not considered 'high art' by the interviewees (there was, for instance, one piece of art that could be considered a part of a cartoon and one photograph), they all were part of the Finnish National Gallery's collections. Some pieces, such as Ferdinand von Wright's *Taistelevat metsot (The Fighting Grouses)* (1886), are so iconic and well known that it is nearly impossible for any Finn not to have seen it—it appears on t-shirts, magnets, posters and so on. The resistance discourse was full of different kinds of critical jokes and 'pleasantries' regarding the art photos. In Focus Group 7 with regulars of a local bar in a small city in the north of Finland, the interviewees said that they would only hang *Taistelevat metsot* on the toilet wall. Marko, the 47-year-old farmer, describes Matti Sainio's black-and-white photograph *Suru ilman mustia vaatteita (Sorrow without Black Clothes)* (1961), a somewhat melancholic picture of a grandfather and a granddaughter in a small boat of the northern Lake Inarinjärvi, in the following way: 'If that isn't a boat for smuggling moonshine! The motor is fuelled up, now come on and hurry up to Estonia to collect the cargo. Great picture. I would not put it on the wall'. In addition to the art photos, another channel for aversion is opera, mentioned by many interviewees and aptly summarised by Mimosa:

> RH: What feels repulsive about it?
> Mimosa: That crowing sound.
> RH: It's only the singing that annoys you?
> Mimosa: Yeah.
> RH: So those costumes and so on...?
> Mimosa: I could watch the theatre, usually they have that theatre part, I could watch it in silence mode, or if it would have classical music in the background, but when they start crowing in there, I'm like, I can't tolerate it.
> (Mimosa, 37, cleaner)

In fact, some of the aesthetical boundaries are so strong that they remind of destruction fantasies. The farmer Marko is very upset that an acquaintance of his often brings and recommends him books: 'Helena often rams all these books down my throat and (…) I just bin them. I don't do anything with them'. A very similar discourse is found in Focus Group 2 with the vocational school male students, when asked whether they receive any magazines at home:

Otso: I don't even open it, I just always throw it into the sauna stove.
Vilho: Same here—happens with that newspaper of the Electrical Workers' Union, my mom always says something like, 'Hey, this arrived'. My only thought is, hey, it's a great firelighter.
(Focus Group 2, male students at a vocational school)

Aesthetical Upward Boundaries: Case Marketta
Marketta is a nearly 70-year-old pensioner who lives in the working-class suburbs of Helsinki. Her profile (urban and with little education) has been especially difficult to recruit, so she is recruited through a research agency. Marketta is very interested in receiving the compensation (a gift card for a local supermarket chain) and much less interested in the interview itself, which she openly shows. We meet at a free meeting space at the central library of Helsinki.
Marketta has had a tumultuous life: she grew up in the countryside with farmer parents and, after completing the (very short at the time) compulsory education, moved to the capital, finished some courses and worked in a number of miscellaneous low-skilled jobs: in a restaurant, in a hospital, in an elderly home, as a security guard at a supermarket and later as a home assistant, a job from which she had to retire early because she had a severe work injury. Marketta's personal life has been equally turbulent: she was a single mother of five children and had to support them all by working seven days a week in random jobs. She became annoyed when asked about the children's hobbies ('who knows what they were doing, they were just at home all the time'). Perhaps the most dramatic feature in her life is that she does not have proper meals unless there happens to be a socially provided meal somewhere that day. On other days, at home, she eats whatever there is in the cupboard ('I eat what I eat. Buns, bread, sausage').
Marketta answers almost all questions curtly, without elaborating on anything even when asked to, and is clearly annoyed by any men-

(*continued*)

(continued)

tion of high culture. Opera reminds her of 'a lady screaming the iron up her ass', and the violins of classical music feel as if they were 'scraping' her ears. Reading books for her is like 'drinking tar'; as did many others, she hated being forced to read at school. When asked what reading she would choose from the library we are in, she says: 'Listen, I have no idea what they have here, and I could not be bothered'. Her standard answer to nearly all the questions is 'not interested'.

Marketta withdraws from almost any cultural participation. She does not go to pubs ('No'), museums ('Not interested'), sports events ('No thanks'), marketplaces ('No money, everything is too expensive there') or cafés ('I get my coffee at home, no need to buy it anywhere'). Nevertheless, being on pension, she has been able to afford some leisure pursuits: she has joined a pensioners' association that offers highly discounted prices for events. She has also gone on some organised bus trips around the world, but always looking for bargains and bringing her own dried food with her.

Marketta's case represents well the extremely heavy aesthetical boundaries present in the resistance discourse. Her attitude is an example par excellence of a nearly physical aesthetic intolerance of and aversion towards other tastes—as Bourdieu famously formulated it, 'tastes are perhaps first and foremost distastes, disgust provoked by horror or visceral intolerance ("sick-making") of the tastes of others' (Bourdieu 1984/1979, 56).

Many scholars have argued that morality is a key dimension in cultural boundaries and that moral and cultural boundaries are often entangled (Harrits and Pedersen 2019; Jarness and Flemmen 2019; Vassenden and Jonvik 2021) In their interviews with Norwegian people low in the class hierarchy, Jarness and Flemmen (2019) noticed that upward boundary-drawing was mostly linked to moral criteria of evaluation and that aesthetical criteria were more related to downward boundary-drawing. In my data, downward aesthetical boundaries were only drawn in the affirmation discourse. Meanwhile, upward moral boundaries were very common, and as in the case of Jarness and Flemmen (2019), they were often mixed with aesthetical upward boundaries, creating a category of 'pretentious snobbery' that was first and foremost aesthetically unpleasant (ugly, disgusting) but also morally dubious (expensive, unnecessary). A typical example was eating, perhaps because it is such a concrete everyday cultural practice:

RH: Any other foods you dislike?
Melissa: Well, maybe these kinds of pretentious things, clams and spinal cords whatever thing it is or squids or this kind of ethnic stuff, no. (…)
RH: What makes you dislike them especially?
Melissa: Perhaps the fact that they have not been made… that you kind of don't know how they have been made and what they have. So no. It's best to make your food yourself, so you know what it has and what you are eating.
(Melissa, NA, disability pension)

Anniina (talking about what restaurants she would not visit): Well the kind of places that only have lots of seafood, those I can't… (…) I'm definitely not going to eat any kind of slimy clams [laughs]. (…) I've tried, and nothing went down and came back up as quickly as when I tried that slimy oyster or what the hell it was (makes a vomiting sound)

RH: Where have you tried that kind of food?
Anniina: Well, when I went to cook training it was part of the thing (…) I tell you nothing has ever gone down and come back up as quickly (makes a spitting sound). They are not my thing, why pay a billion of euros without any reason for this kind of clams and disgusting snails and other things, I just can't do it. Those kinds of places – I can avoid them, I don't need them.
(Anniina, 39, unemployed)

In sum, upward aesthetical boundaries are a central part of the resistance discourse—harsh boundaries are drawn against a cultural-aesthetical milieu that mainly consists of the usual suspects of highbrow culture (opera, ballet, fine dining and so on), which are considered revolting and even physically intolerable. The aversion was displayed very openly throughout the interviews via physical imitations of vomiting, which again comes very close to Bourdieu's notion of 'visceral intolerance' towards other classes' tastes (Bourdieu 1984/1979, 56). In any case, aesthetical boundaries are not enough to understand the intensity of the upward boundaries drawn in the resistance discourse. That is why the next subchapter will deepen our understanding by scrutinising the upward moral boundaries.

A Quest for Equality: Moral Upward Boundaries

Upward moral boundaries are a significant part of the logic of the resistance discourse. People perceived as 'higher' in hierarchies are sometimes described as not only 'snobs', but also as 'queue-jumpers', 'hypocritical moralists' or 'picky and fastidious'. In general, hierarchies are felt in the flesh, and the people perceived to be rubbing them in the interviewees' faces were openly despised. This reflects well the literature sharing the view that moral standards can work for the underprivileged groups as alternative ways of building worth when economic and cultural resources are too scarce for this task (Harrits and Pedersen 2019; Lamont 2000). Therefore, the symbolic boundaries drawn by people low in the hierarchies could be interpreted as 'a defensive need to maintain a sense of dignity and self-worth against the background of one's low position in the class structure' (Jarness and Flemmen 2019, 177). In Jarness' and Flemmen's interviews with the lower classes in Norway, moral boundaries worked differently when drawn upwards and downwards: upwards, the boundaries were 'usurpationary', while downwards, they were 'exclusionary', highlighting that the upper classes' perceived good moral qualities, such as being kind, made them tolerable in the eyes of the lower classes (Jarness and Flemmen 2019).

In the resistance discourse identified in my interviews, the interviewees clearly recognised themselves as belonging to the losing side. This cannot be described simply as a 'sense of one's place' which Bourdieu coins as an unconscious approbation of the existence of hierarchies 'which leads one to exclude oneself from the goods, persons, places and so forth from which one is excluded' (Bourdieu 1984/1979, 471). In the case of the resistance discourse, this process is not unconscious but, instead, very conscious indeed. Many interviewees described the feeling of having a lower status than others, which made them uncomfortable, humiliated and angry. For instance, Minna, the manual worker on maternity leave whom we met earlier, is very annoyed by the hierarchies at her workplace: although she thought that the coffee room should be a place in which equality between workers reigns, the people working in the offices of the company automatically expected her, as technical personnel, to make coffee for others. This annoys her tremendously:

Even if I had more education, even if I would be the shopkeeper myself, I would not like it, I would not be like, 'I am the captain of this ship', but

rather like… 'If we do this together, everybody does it together'. I don't like this unequal thing, hierarchy, I don't like it at all.
(Minna, 38, manual worker)

Eero, a 30-year-old kiosk worker, is permanently irritated with the customers of the kiosk who, in his opinion, treat him like scum, think too much of themselves and take too many liberties. Eero's day of his dreams is in fact a subversion of the extant state of affairs:

> I would like to be (…) a genuine dickhead, a totally genuine dickhead. If it were possible for one day, I would like to park my car in the disabled parking lot, pass everybody in the queue, shout at my mother, be the extreme that I unfortunately have to encounter. (…) I would overdo everything. I might just push a wheelchair into the ground and throw it away. That kind of thing. I would overdo everything, just everything, I would do anything I can just for the joy of being able to do it. No one could do anything. If a car would be parked wrongly, I would make dents into it.
> (Eero, 30, kiosk worker)

These depictions are only inches away from upward symbolic moral boundaries. The people 'higher up' in the hierarchy from the likes of Minna and Eero are easily described as self-satisfied and smug complainers, the 'moral police', picky and fussy and so on. Much of the resistance discourse is based on the idea that cultural participation itself is a luxury that not everyone can afford, which points, again, beyond Bourdieu's idea of the 'taste of necessity' (Bourdieu 1984/1979, 380). For instance, the men interviewed in Focus Group 5 with an association of unemployed people continuously stated that rich people's cultural practices become picky basically because they can afford to choose. As one of the participants expressed this sentiment: 'Hunger has basically taught me that if there is a tight situation, life will teach you. That's how pickiness will go away. But if you are really very hungry, you will definitely become less self-satisfied'. The kiosk worker Eero has a similar tone when describing the restaurants he would not like to visit:

> Maybe some kind of vegetarian place. Not because it has vegetarian food but because of the people who go there, because those people boast about how vegetarian they are, and I just cannot tolerate it. (…) It's because of their self-satisfaction mostly, they cannot enjoy the food, they have to tell

that they've spent fifteen years eating only sprouts, that ruins my appetite. That self-satisfaction that is included in the whole thing.

Finally, the farmer Marko, whom we know from the prologue of this chapter, is in general critical of fussy people who complain too much. Marko speaks fondly of his many 'field cars', unregistered and uninspected cars which are not allowed to be driven on official roads but that some people, mainly in the countryside, use for tinkering and fixing or sometimes driving in closed rally events. What annoys him is the other peoples' criticism and what he labels as 'environmental craziness':

> Well, here and there I've heard that if they [the field cars] start to accumulate in your yard, your neighbours will start complaining that they leak oil and all that and that they look ugly, nag, nag, nag. It's this kind of modern environmental craziness, it's become largely like that nowadays.

The flipside of these upward moral boundaries is a strong call for equality. There seems to be a consensus in the resistance discourse that hierarchies for the sake of hierarchies are wrong and that no one's cultural practices should be criticised without reason: in short, what seems to be a certain restoration of the honour of egalitarian values. Many interviewees close to the resistance discourse have rather liberal political values: they actively follow politics online, but they are intolerant of people who loudly dominate the debates. For instance, Max, a 39-year-old unemployed man with a background in many different manual jobs, follows politics both online and by reading magazines and is highly critical of debates that he feels are extreme:

> Max (speaking about his reading preferences): I think mostly I like to read these kinds of societal, political, that kind of writings. Politics has started to interest me more.
> RH: You ever comment on the writings yourself?
> Max: No, I usually don't comment myself, those questions related to politics become so easily exaggerated that I try to keep myself out of those conversations.
> RH: So you just follow?
> Max: Yes I mostly do, usually I like to follow factual discussions rather than debates with expressions like 'libtard' and 'rightard' [laughs], I'm really allergic to that kind of stuff.

Eero, the 30-year-old kiosk worker, takes this position a little further: like Max, he follows political debates online, but he often fights back and comments on debates that he finds stupid. Like he formulates it:

> My sense of justice is so strong that I just don't give in. I have zero tolerance for that kind of stupidity. I cannot just accept that evolution has developed us to this point in which we can build anything, we have technology and all that. (…) I'm just allergic to that stupidity. (…) Well, I can accept that I don't know things, that's not stupidity. But if you choose not to accept facts, that's incomprehensible, that's real stupidity (…) in my opinion. Sounds bad, but that's how I see it.

When asked where he thinks all the online hate speech stems from, he says:

> Probably it's because, you have problems, and you must offload them on something else. And well, as we just had this immigration thing, it could be that their culture is so different, and you see such a little bit of it, it's an easy target as there is so much negative things about it in the media, it's so easy to jump on that same train.

Finally, an interview excerpt with young women studying at a vocational school is worth quoting at length, as they really are only able to communicate their desire for 'democratic' cultural practices after ruling out what they consider *morally* wrong:

> RH: You have any other ideas about what kinds of books or magazines you would hate?
> Katja: I don't know, probably something that is communist…
> Sonja: Yeah. [laughs]
> RH: OK. What do you mean more specifically?
> Katja: I don't know, kind of, I don't know if you could call it brainwashing.
> Sonja: Yeah.
> Katja: But well (…) I don't understand absolutely anything about politics, but I like more this current model that we have now in Finland, that's why communism came into my mind. [laughs] This democracy we have in Finland, I like it.
> RH: So you dislike something like pamphlets or something like that?
> Katja: What's a pamphlet?
> RH: I don't know, information (…) of the ideological kind.

Katja: Well, I can't call it brainwashing but I don't like that they just tell me 'this is how things are'. I want a really very good argumentation for things.
(Focus Group 1, students at a vocational school)

Upward Moral Boundaries: Case Eero
Eero is a 30-year-old man living in a big city in the north of Finland. I recruit him through a local Facebook group, and he is instantly keen on being interviewed. After negotiating with his boss about what day he could take off from his work at a kiosk, we meet at a cosy Vietnamese café that he has suggested.

Eero has worked in different customer service positions since he was 15: in telemarketing, in cafés and lunch places and in a super-market. His life is very much defined by his current job at the kiosk. The job makes him so tired that in his free time and holidays he mostly wants to stay at home alone, usually fixing computers ('if I spend a couple of days on my own and practically lock myself into my apartment (…) I get more energy'). The work is exhausting also mentally, especially because so many people behave badly and Eero feels the need to keep them under control ('sometimes I'm very close to blowing up and punching someone in the face').

Eero's cultural practices are, in general, typical for a young man of his generation, and some are, again, tightly related to his identity in customer service: he likes heavy music ('I guess it is a counterbalance for all that joyfulness and positivity that they expect from me at work') and reality TV ('the previous kiosk owner was an ex-police, I always heard police stories from him') and is open-minded about food ('Chili sandwiches or garlic sandwiches or Thai food, I always try something new. Usually, I fail four times, and then I succeed').

Eero engages little in highbrow-oriented participation. He reads sometimes (his favourites are *The Hitchhiker's Guide to the Galaxy* and *A Series of Unfortunate Events*) but never goes to classical music concerts, to the opera or the ballet (as a child he was often 'dragged' to the theatre by his mother). Still, he draws no upward aesthetical boundaries. Instead, he draws strong upward moral boundaries upwards, and even those are linked to Eero's job. For instance, he

(*continued*)

(continued)

finds that he cannot go to bars or be seen drunk as he works in the public eye ('I don't like the idea that I would fool around out there drunk, and customers would see me wasted'). He is indignant about the bad behaviours of many customers and has started a one-man 'restoration of discipline' at the kiosk: 'If there is no respect for the salesperson, there is no salesperson'.

This attitude sometimes pours out as hatred of all the hierarchies around Eero. When I ask him about the day of his dreams, he imagines a scene in which he would be 'in control': he would take the wheelchairs away from the invalids, slander passers-by (and his mother) and discipline cars for parking wrongly. At the same time, he invests effort in putting people right on various internet forums that he follows ('there are few extremes in Finland, and there are two possibilities – either you are with them or against them (...) if some people in those organisations try to bring up a point without any point, typically I start to shout about it at them'). In Eero's case, moral boundaries are predominant at the expense of nearly insignificant aesthetical boundaries. In this sense, Eero is a good example of how moral boundaries can become essential for understanding how cultural distinction works (Lamont 1992). Furthermore, his case exemplifies well *how* exactly moral standards can become an alternative for showing worth when there is a lack of economic and/or cultural resources (Jarness and Flemmen 2019; Lamont 2000).

We have seen that moral boundaries directed upwards are an essential part of the resistance discourse. The interviewees that felt that highbrow-oriented cultural practices were distant and sometimes even repulsive often considered the 'upper' groups morally dubious: picky, fastidious and badly behaved. This echoes well with Jarness and Flemmen's (2019) findings about the fact that there is a symbolic market for a certain kindness of the upper groups among the lower classes: as long as the upper groups are perceived of as 'ordinary' or 'nice', the hierarchy is not challenged. My interviewees, even many of the most unprivileged ones, expressed feelings that went even beyond this point: they had strong ideals about abandoning hierarchies and about achieving equality. The kiosk worker Eero happens to quote the famous Jantelagen (Sandemose 1933/1936) almost to the letter when talking about the kiosk customers: 'Many have started to behave exemplarily when someone has reminded them from time to time that, "hey, you are dealing with people here, you are not more special than anyone else, now try to behave"'.

CONCLUSION: RESISTING HEGEMONIC TASTES AND LIFESTYLES

The resistance discourse is strongly inclined towards popular and everyday cultural participation. In unison with a resistance towards highbrow-oriented culture (which comes out, as we have seen, through feelings of unfamiliarity and discomfort and especially aesthetical and moral upward boundaries), there is also popular and everyday participation, such as going to popular music concerts, watching television, browsing the internet, hunting, going berry-picking and so on. One might ask: In that case, why was this discourse labelled "resistance'? Because the core of the discourse is based on an opposition and resistance to the norm of highbrow-oriented cultural participation. The affirmation discourse embraces and strives after this norm, the functionality discourse treats it with indifference, and the resistance discourse is opposed to it. This opposition is related to a recognition of one's own lower standing in the hierarchy and the identification of cultural capital as something of which one is dispossessed. This leads to feelings of being an outsider and being left out—that is, to a modern version of Willis's 'caged resentment which always stops just short of outright confrontation' (1977/2017, 120), a rejection of cultural practices considered middle-class, though always from an underdog's position.

It is probably only logical that the many methodological challenges of the interviews were especially related to the resistance discourse. The interviewees close to the resistance discourse often expressed their discomfort and resistance, directed both against the formal interview, the topic of the interview—cultural practices—and the interviewer herself. This has been extensively touched upon in a previous paper (Heikkilä and Katainen 2021), but to summarise it should be said that the different forms of counter-talk appearing in the interviews could be interpreted as expressions of resistance to neoliberal accounts of economic and cultural success (Lamont 2000). One can also conclude that paying closer attention to the parts of the interviews that initially appeared failed—'obscene' jokes, mocking, deviations from the topic and so on—was key for understanding the different processes of meaning-making, class distinction and boundary-drawing.

The boundaries drawn in the resistance discourse were basically all directed upwards. They were either aesthetical (directed against highbrow-oriented cultural participation and items described as disgusting, intolerable or ridiculous) or moral (directed against people considered snobbish, hypocritical or picky). In the underprivileged groups interviewed by Jarness and Flemmen, all upward boundaries were mostly moral (Jarness and Flemmen 2019). Here, the differences to my study are twofold. First, I found clear and strong aesthetical upward boundaries that seemed to repeat the classical patterns of strong aesthetical intolerance described by Bourdieu (1984/1979). Second, and much more importantly, the Finnish resistance discourse does not draw symbolic boundaries *downwards*, unlike its Norwegian counterpart. Here, there are no signs that 'one part of the working class is content to describe another section of the working class as feckless and without taste' (Bennett et al. 2009, 211) or that lower classes would use the same boundaries that are drawn against them to maintain respectability (Skeggs 1997).

How, then, is the resistance discourse related to egalitarianism? There are clear signs of anti-institutional sentiments and even of anti-establishment ideas (Gest 2016), whereby the 'system' has stopped working for underprivileged groups, which is one of the 'deep stories' Kantola et al. (2022) identified in their recent study on the Finnish society. Many interviewees felt that their cultural participation was worth nothing in the eyes of the groups higher up in the hierarchy. To summarise, there is a profound awareness of exploitation (Skeggs and Loveday 2012) in the resistance discourse. There is thus a strong pull towards the 'fatalistic worldview' that De Keere (2020) describes as dismissive, anti-establishment and non-conformist—therefore, for people close to the resistance discourse, 'the way to counteract and survive this situation is by not abiding by the rules and instead emphasizing one's own hedonism, straightforwardness and non-hypocrisy' (De Keere 2020, 5). However, this is not the whole story. The resistance discourse also expresses a desire to subvert the hierarchy and to establish equality more strongly regarding cultural practices and beyond. People close to the resistance discourse are aware of their low status, but they call for being treated as equals and are not keen to naturalise or legitimise class inequalities through moral judgements (see Jarness and Flemmen 2019). In this sense, they still lean more towards more collective values of egalitarianism, which De Keere (2020) defines using a distinction between the cultural and the economic lower classes, linking the former to egalitarianism and the latter to a fatalistic worldview. This is also corroborated by the finding that there are no downward symbolic boundaries drawn in the resistance discourse. One could thus argue that in the resistance discourse, which clearly is situated the furthest away from normative cultural participation, there is some idea of an intra-class solidarity and a desire for egalitarianism.

References

Bennett T, Savage M, Silva E, Warde A, Gayo-Cal M and Wright D (2009) *Culture, Class, Distinction*. London: Routledge.
Bourdieu P (1984/1979) *Distinction. A Social Critique of the Judgment of Taste*. London: Routledge & Kegan Paul.
Bourdieu P (1986) The Forms of Capital. In J Richardson (ed) *Handbook of Theory and Research for the Sociology of Education*. New York: Greenwood, pp. 241–258.
Bourdieu P (1993) *The Field of Cultural Production. Essays on Art and Literature*. New York: Columbia Press.
Bourdieu P and Darbel A (1991) *The Love of Art: European Art Museums and Their Public*. Cambridge, UK: Polity.
Bourdieu P and Passeron JC (1979) *The Inheritors: French Students and Their Relation to Culture*. Chicago, IL: University of Chicago Press.
De Keere K (2020) Finding the moral space: Rethinking morality, social class and worldviews. *Poetics* 79: 101415.
Flemmen, M, Jarness, V and Rosenlund, L (2018) Social space and cultural class divisions: The forms of capital and contemporary lifestyle differentiation. *British Journal of Sociology* 69(1): 124–153.
Friedman S and Kuipers, G (2013). The divisive power of humour: Comedy, taste and symbolic boundaries. *Cultural Sociology* 7(2): 179–195.
Gest J (2016). *The new minority. White working class politics in an age of immigration and inequality*. Oxford: Oxford University Press.
Harrits GS and Pedersen HH (2019) Symbolic Class Struggles and the Intersection of Socioeconomic, Cultural and Moral Categorisations. *Sociology* 53(5): 861–878.
Heikkilä R (2021) The slippery slope of cultural non-participation: Orientations of participation among the potentially passive. *European Journal of Cultural Studies* 24: 202–219.
Heikkilä R and Katainen A (2021) Counter-talk as symbolic boundary drawing: Challenging legitimate cultural practices in individual and focus group interviews in the lower regions of social space. *Sociological Review* 69: 1029–1050.
Hochschild AR (2016) *Strangers in Their Own Land*. New York: The New Press.

Jarness V and Flemmen M (2019) A struggle on two fronts: Boundary drawing in the lower region of the social space and the symbolic market for "down-to-earthness". *British Journal of Sociology* 70: 166–189.

Jones O (2016) *Chavs. The demonization of the working class.* London: Verso.

Kantola A, Aaltonen S, Haikkola L, Junnilainen L, Luhtakallio E, Patana P, Timonen J and Tuominen P (2022) *Kahdeksan kuplan Suomi. Yhteiskunnan muutosten syvät tarinat [Finland's eight bubbles. The deep stories of societal changes].* Gaudeamus: Helsinki.

Kuipers G (2015) *Good humour, bad taste: A sociology of the joke.* Boston: de Gruyter.

Lamont M (1992) *Money, Morals and Manners: The Culture of the French and American Upper Middle Classes.* Chicago: University of Chicago Press.

Lamont M (2000) *Dignity of Working Men. Morality and the Boundaries of Race, Class, and Immigration.* Cambridge: Harvard University Press.

Lamont M (2018) Addressing Recognition Gaps: Destigmatization and the Reduction of Inequality. *American Sociological Review* 83(3): 419–444.

Loveday V (2015) Working-Class Participation, Middle-Class Aspiration? Value, Upward Mobility and Symbolic Indebtedness in Higher Education. *The Sociological Review* 63(3): 570–588.

Miles A and Gibson L (2016) Everyday participation and cultural value. *Cultural Trends* 25(3): 151–157.

Ollivier M (2008) Modes of openness to cultural diversity. Humanist, populist, practical, and indifferent. *Poetics* 36 (2–3): 120–147.

Purhonen S, Gronow J, Heikkilä R, Kahma N, Rahkonen K, Toikka A (2014) *Suomalainen maku: Kulttuuripääoma, kulutus ja elämäntyylien sosiaalinen eriytyminen [Finnish taste: Cultural capital, consumption and the social differentiation of lifestyles].* Helsinki: Gaudeamus.

Sandemose A (1933/1936). *A Fugitive Crosses his Tracks.* New York: Alfred A. Knopp.

Savage M, Cunningham N, Devine F, Friedman S, Laurison D, McKenzie L, Miles A, Snee H and Wakeling P (2015) *Social Class in the 21st Century.* London: Pelican.

Skeggs B (1997) *Formations of Class and Gender. Becoming respectable.* London: Sage.

Skeggs B and Loveday V (2012) Struggles for Value: Value Practices, Injustice, Judgment, Affect and the Idea of Class. *The British Journal of Sociology* 63(3): 472–490.

Tyler I (2013) *Revolting Subjects: Social Abjection and Resistance in Neoliberal Britain.* London: Zed Books.

Vassenden A and Jonvik M (2021) Live and let live? Morality in symbolic boundaries across different cultural areas. *Current Sociology.* Available at: https://doi.org/10.1177/00113921211034892 (Accessed 21 August 2022).

Willis P (1977/2017) *Learning to Labour: How Working-Class Kids Get Working Class Jobs.* London: Routledge.

PART III

Paving the Way for Future Debates

CHAPTER 8

Conclusion

Abstract This chapter summarises the main findings. First, cultural non-participation is first and foremost a methodological artefact. Second, cultural non-participation (in highbrow-oriented activities) is only in some cases 'compensated' by informal social of kin-based participation. Rather, there are generally very active people and people who mostly engage in everyday pursuits. Third, the three main categories of talking about cultural non-participation in Finland were the following three: 'affirmation', 'functionality' and 'resistance' discourses. The chapter then discusses the problematic role of cultural policy in subverting existing hierarchies. After discussing briefly the main limitations, the chapter concludes that the best possibilities for equalising or at least balancing cultural participation lie in an equal society and that understanding this is key in our societies characterised by cultural divides.

Keywords Cultural participation • Cultural non-participation • Affirmation • Functionality • Resistance • Cultural equality

© The Author(s) 2022, corrected publication 2023   139
R. Heikkilä, *Understanding Cultural Non-Participation in an Egalitarian Context*, Palgrave Studies in Cultural Participation,
https://doi.org/10.1007/978-3-031-18865-7_8

Main Findings

In this book, I set out to understand cultural non-participation in Finland, a relatively egalitarian context. I asked how the cultural participation of the hypothetically 'non-participating' groups is constituted in Finland and what kinds of boundaries the people who belong to these groups draw when discussing their cultural participation. For this purpose, I interviewed 40 individuals and 9 focus groups whose background factors—such as low education, living in a small place, working in a manual job or being outside of the labour market, living in northern or eastern Finland and so on—predicted low cultural participation.

The first main finding was that non-participation in culture is first and foremost a methodological artefact: the fact that most surveys on cultural practices are based on highbrow-oriented items obscures the fact that people who look like non-participants when only highbrow items are taken into consideration do, in fact, have active lives filled with popular and mundane cultural practices. Culturally speaking, not a single one of my interviewees was entirely 'passive'—all participated in cultural activities of some kind. This methodological short-sightedness has been widely criticised as derogatory and as a way of effacing from view the life-worlds of different underprivileged classes (see Flemmen et al. 2018; Ollivier 2008; Savage et al. 2015). There is a wide consensus that the labelling of cultural non-participation as disinterest or laziness (see Stevenson 2019) is degrading.

The everyday participation debate has, in many ways, come to the rescue here by pointing out that informal and mundane forms of culture are also valuable (Back 2015; Ebrey 2016; Gilmore 2017; Miles and Gibson 2016). In the same vein, it has been suggested that the lack of highbrow-oriented cultural participation can be compensated for by different kinds of forms of informal, home-based, vernacular and local participation (Bennett et al. 2009). However, in the light of my empirical data, it seems like this is only a part of the whole story. My second main finding was that cultural non-participation (in highbrow-oriented activities) is only in some cases 'compensated' for by informal, social or kin-based participation. Rather, although all interviewees do exhibit at least everyday participation, it was possible to detect a certain polarisation between general activity and a withdrawal from canonised forms of cultural participation: at one end of the spectrum, there are people who are active in highbrow-oriented, popular and everyday cultural activities, while at the other end, there are people who mostly engage in everyday pursuits only and who sometimes have hostile attitudes towards established forms of cultural participation. This picture further confirms the pattern revealed by many recent quantitative studies (Heikkilä and Lindblom 2022; Prieur and Savage 2013; Purhonen et al. 2014; Savage et al. 2015; Weingartner and Rössel 2019). This polarisation emerges when looking more closely at the discourses of my interviewees. My third finding was that these discourses fell into the following three categories: these were 'affirmation', 'functionality' and 'resistance'.

The affirmation discourse includes elements from both highbrow-oriented, popular and everyday milieus. It is characterised particularly by its emphasis on the value of culture per se, the importance of remaining active and a belief in the positive or even transformative power of cultural participation, all of which can be interpreted as a version of cultural goodwill, described as 'the most unconditional testimonies of cultural docility' (Bourdieu 1984/1979, 321). In the affirmation discourse, while there are no upward boundaries drawn, downward boundaries are both aesthetical (directed against lowbrow cultural practices in general) and moral (directed against laziness and non-participation). One could argue that the affirmation discourse, at least to some degree, recognises the hegemonic discourses of the participation norm and exhibits acquiescence towards it. Thus, this discourse comes close to Bourdieu's idea that symbolic violence requires the acquiescence of the dominated party and that such acquiescence is actually the principal mechanism of social reproduction and keeping up the hegemony (Bourdieu 1998). This interpretation can also help us understand why the affirmation discourse seemed to be much more prevalent among women than men (see also Jarness and Flemmen 2019). The affirmation discourse is situated close to the core ideals of egalitarianism: there is a strong feeling of being a sovereign member of different societal levels and of being entitled to participate in highbrow-oriented culture. Finally, there is also the belief that highbrow-oriented cultural participation can provide cultural capital which, in turn, is capable of providing returns, at least hypothetically.

The functionality discourse mainly consists of elements from the popular and everyday milieus. It is characterised by a practical, functional and thus extremely personal relationship with cultural participation: cultural participation serves everyday life by facilitating relaxation and wellness, and therefore, the discourse is characterised by a modest and indifferent attitude towards cultural participation. This finding reflects, for instance,

Ollivier's argument on 'indifferent openness' (Ollivier 2008) whereby openness to all kinds of cultural practices is emphasised although one's actual cultural practices are narrow. There are also similarities with Vassenden and Jonvik's (2019) finding that their Norwegian interviewees with less education were largely indifferent to cultural capital and secure about their own lifestyles. Unlike the affirmation discourse, the functionality discourse draws upward boundaries which all are aesthetical: they are directed against what are perceived as impractical or non-functional cultural practices. The core of the functionality discourse consists in representing these aesthetical upward boundaries as individual choices, as not 'my thing'. This strategy could be interpreted as a weak sign of egalitarianism: although aesthetical boundaries are drawn upwards against cultural practices perceived as remote and alien, there is a strong tolerance of others' cultural practices without signs of anti-elitism.

The resistance discourse, like the functionality discourse, rests on elements from the popular and everyday milieus. Unlike the two previous discourses, however, its relationship with culture is characterised by hostility, defiance and a sometimes even a certain search for conflict. There is cultural participation, but highbrow-oriented culture is seen as having very little or no intrinsic value. The resistance discourse is largely marked by feelings of being left behind, a finding that echoes the empirical results of other scholars who have described the feelings of loss of power and resentment that many contemporary low-standing groups have (Gest 2016; Hochschild 2016). In the resistance discourse, two kinds of upward boundaries are drawn: aesthetical (drawn against classical highbrow-oriented cultural practices, perceived as both disgusting and ridiculous) and moral (drawn against snobbishness and hierarchies in general). These boundaries can be understood as a strategy of building and maintaining worth in a context of low cultural, social and economic resources (Harrits and Pedersen 2019; Jarness and Flemmen 2019; Lamont 2000). The connection of the resistance discourse to egalitarianism is twofold. On the one hand, there is a strong awareness of exploitation (Skeggs and Loveday 2012) and, therefore, a tendency to adopt a dismissive and non-conformist 'fatalistic worldview' (De Keere 2020). On the other hand, in the resistance discourse, there is an explicit wish to return to a more egalitarian scenario—the interviewees closest to the resistance discourse express their desire to be treated as equals instead of following naturalised class inequalities (see Jarness and Flemmen 2019). Bearing in mind that the resistance discourse does not draw any downward boundaries, it could be speculated that among the underprivileged groups interviewed in Finland, there is some intra-class solidarity and a wish for more egalitarianism.

These findings, which show highly differentiated discourses regarding cultural practices within a relatively homogeneous group in an egalitarian context, may seem surprising. Nevertheless, it is possible that a highly egalitarian context can 'conceal, maintain and even help to shape, the hierarchical structures of society' (Jarness 2015, 68), which makes 'falling out of the reach of the system' an even more stigmatising experience.

THE PROBLEMATIC ROLE OF CULTURAL POLICY IN SUBVERTING EXISTING HIERARCHIES

Although all my interviewees actively engaged in *some* kind of cultural participation, my research echoes the results of quantitative studies with large representative samples: a large part of people with low class positions withdraw partly or totally from publicly funded, highbrow-oriented culture (García-Álvarez et al. 2007; Heikkilä 2021; Katz-Gerro and Jaeger 2013; Purhonen et al. 2014; Taylor 2016; Willekens and Lievens 2016). This kind of scenario represents a challenge to the kind of public cultural policy whose basic ideal claims that cultural participation is beneficial and that the public subvention of culture equalises the participation of underprivileged groups.

It has been argued that the fundamental elements of public policy are skewed in multiple ways. First, funding typically 'entails a redistribution of resources upwards, towards those who are already most privileged' (Miles and Sullivan 2012, 321). A typical practical example of this tendency is that, since the advent of neoliberal policies and the decentralisation of cultural policy in the 1990s, even in countries with traditionally strong national cultural policies, governments have had to look for new sources of funding for public culture, such as national lotteries (Dubois 2015). For instance, in Finland, three-quarters of the budget for public culture comes from the national lottery funds, which are susceptible to economic fluctuations (Häyrynen 2006). Thus, it can be argued that the public money for funding highbrow-oriented culture comes disproportionately from the lower classes, also in Finland.

Second, it has been suggested that cultural policymaking itself is biased because its voices basically come from and therefore favour different elite groups (Jancovich 2017; Stevenson 2019). Beyond these practical asymmetries, it is an open question whether public funding of culture can actually modify the existing social hierarchies by lowering the cultural participation threshold of underprivileged groups (see Belfiore 2002) or whether public funding of culture ends up reproducing existing social hierarchies by supporting cultural activities that are mostly associated with higher-status groups (Bjørnsen 2012; Feder and Katz-Gerro 2015).

Belfiore and Bennett (2008) show that many key motivations and ideals of cultural policy, such as the arts being 'good for you' or having transformative positive powers, are in fact age-old. In a similar manner, Belfiore has argued that one of the central ideals behind cultural policy is the belief that cultural participation can alleviate inequalities and even ease complicated social problems related to health, crime, social integration and so on (Belfiore 2002). In the recent decades, there has been plenty of critical discussion on the evaluation and performance measurement of cultural policy in terms of whether the effects of cultural participation can really be 'measured': it has been argued that 'public cultural expenses are gradually viewed in terms of investments from which economic impacts are expected' (Dubois 2015, 13). This 'cult of measuring' is argued to be driven by the perceived positive social impact of cultural participation (Belfiore and Bennett 2010; Bunting et al. 2019) and the fact that cultural policy has been penetrated by neoliberal ideals. Some scholars have claimed that this development, in fact, legitimises the institutions receiving public funding and bolsters the argument on the 'problem' of cultural non-participation (Stevenson 2013, 2019). One can argue that this process leads to a certain vicious circle in which highbrow-oriented cultural institutions are supported through public funding in order to attract larger publics, while the funding received further legitimises these institutions and ends up alienating them even more from the groups whose participation has been low since the start. It has even been suggested that cultural policy models as we know them have reached the end of the road: cultural policy has not succeeded in 'democratising' culture as promised, a central aim and mission of cultural policy since the mid-twentieth century (Mangset 2020). Mangset (2020) further claims that, for instance, public policies have become stagnant in supporting out-of-date cultural institutions and in continuing to see public cultural policy as a national matter even though cultural production, dissemination and supply chains are thoroughly globalised.

The following question remains: How can different public actors implement equal and intelligent cultural policies? The fact that cultural participation seems to be organised along a continuum of participation versus non-participation (Prieur and Savage 2013; Purhonen et al. 2014; Savage et al. 2015; Weingartner and Rössel 2019) reflects the complicated challenge of engaging the people who are most detached from cultural participation. Research shows that different interventions to engage people usually manage to target mainly those who already are potential or existing participants (Jancovich and Ejgod Hansen 2018). A related question is whether the people who participate little in highbrow-oriented culture really even wish to participate more. Bourdieu has suggested that the language of 'deficit' in itself is pointless because the underprivileged classes themselves do not experience a deprivation of culture (Bourdieu and Darbel 1991). Bourdieu's explanation was that only a minority of people can properly benefit from highbrow-oriented cultural participation and that institutions of high art, such as museums, 'betray, in the smallest details of their morphology and their organization, their true function, which is to strengthen the feeling of belonging in some and the feeling of exclusion in others' (Bourdieu 1993, 236). Bourdieu maintains that the attempts to lower the participation thresholds of high arts institutions—for instance, by providing free entrance—is misleading and strengthens the initial inequality of access: 'free entrance is also optional entrance, reserved for those who, endowed with the ability to appropriate the works, have the privilege of using this freedom and who find themselves consequently legitimised in their privilege' (Bourdieu 1993, 237).

In this context, it becomes important to ask who is seen as 'deserving' of certain patterns of (publicly funded) cultural participation. Borrowing from social policy scholarship (Van Oorschot 2000, 2006), cultural policy could, perhaps, be understood as a question of 'deservingness'. For example, Van Oorschot (2000) identified the following deservingness criteria: (1) control over neediness (people considered responsible for their own neediness are not seen as deserving), (2) the level of need (people needing more also deserve more), (3) identity (people considered closer to 'us' are considered more deserving), (4) attitude (the people seen as pleasant, thankful and/or compliant are seen as deserving) and (5) reciprocity (groups that have contributed to 'us' before are seen as more deserving than others). For instance, McKenzie (2015, 171) argues that the working classes themselves recognise well the discourse of the 'deserving poor' and the 'undeserving poor'. When translating these conceptualisations into cultural policy, one could argue that there are groups that see themselves as either 'deserving' or 'undeserving' of the fruits of *cultural* policy and adopt their stances towards cultural participation accordingly. To give another example, Kantola et al. (2022) showed that among the lowest-standing groups, not participating in societal affairs or refraining from, for instance, voting was considered an active operation, a kind of 'weapon of the weak' that materialises in different forms of everyday resistance (Scott 1985).

Finally, going back to the empirical data used in this book and to the idea of egalitarianism: in the Finnish case, is it true, as De Keere argues (2020), that low-standing groups with some cultural capital adhere to egalitarian values the most? The data clearly shows that the discourses indicating some cultural capital (or with favourable attitudes towards it) are close to egalitarian values; these discourses entail the belief that one can participate in and be a part of culture or at least acquire culture and to learn to appreciate it. At the same time, the discourses furthest away from egalitarianism are close to fatalism; they are penetrated by the idea of fall-ing out of the reach of established forms of culture and that most highbrow-oriented forms of cultural participation do not 'speak to one' at all. This attitude is sometimes accompanied by surrender or even defiance and anger—and this is precisely what makes it especially challenging for cultural policies to attract the groups that embrace this kind of attitude.

LIMITATIONS

Like always, there are some limitations to take into account. A central one of them was that in the empirical data, probably very much like in every-day conversations, it was difficult if not impossible to disentangle partici-pation from the other components of cultural practices, namely, taste and knowledge. In the interviews, when people were discussing cultural par-ticipation, they often started talking about taste, and when talking about taste, they typically begun discussing whether they knew certain cultural products. Cultural participation is thus not an island that can be studied in isolation from other areas of culture. In the words of Antoine Hennion, 'Taste is not an attribute, it is not a property (of a thing or of a person), it is an activity. You have to do something in order to listen to music, drink a wine, appreciate an object' (Hennion 2007, 101). The same goes for participation: there is rarely any cultural participation without pre-existing taste or knowledge.

Another limitation is related to the much-debated topic of whether interviews can convey true behaviours (Jerolmack and Khan 2014).

Qualitative research interviews are certainly artificial situations in which the interviewers typically have more power than interviewees (Heikkilä and Katainen 2021) and in which interviewees tend to present themselves according to their choices or abilities (Ollivier 2008). Nonetheless, I maintain that interviews are highly useful in capturing interviewees' life-worlds and can demonstrate how (and whether) different interviewees are able and willing to navigate situations of asymmetrical power relations (Heikkilä and Katainen 2021; Kvale and Brinkmann 2009; Lamont and Swidler 2014). I also argue that qualitative methods entail an important sensitivity that is needed to capture the life-worlds of partly vulnerable groups and to unveil practices that remain invisible to a large part of research. This perspective is especially relevant for research on cultural practices in which the 'domination of survey instrument limits understandings of the everyday cultural field' (Miles and Gibson 2016, 154). Scholars have argued that if we adopt a narrow view of what cultural participation actually is, this will end up narrowing the entire conceptualisation of cultural participation and further reifying highbrow-oriented culture (Milling 2019).

It could be considered a limitation that I formed a theoretical sample based on factors statistically predicting a certain kind of behaviour, in this case low cultural participation, instead of finding people with self-reported low cultural participation and conducting interviews with them. The main reason for this methodological choice was that interviewing people who label themselves as 'passives' and voluntarily participate in an academic study on the topic would probably have produced mostly hostile discourses, as argued in the Introduction to this chapter. Moreover, interviewing people whose backgrounds predict low cultural participation means that one has better chances of going beyond the methodological dilemma related to finding large proportions of 'passives' in nationally representative surveys (Flemmen et al. 2018; Heikkilä 2021; Purhonen et al. 2014), which are often inadequate at representing people's motivations and reasons for participating or not participating in culture (Bunting et al. 2019). Finally, it should be kept in mind that my interviewees belong to the Finnish popular classes (possibly excluded from high culture but not from the rest of the society), a large societal group rather than a muted minority. My results could have looked different, had I included, for instance, people from the Swedish-speaking language minority, who are known to perform better than the language majority on most socio-economic indicators and who possibly exhibit fewer inter-class differences when speaking about cultural practices (Heikkilä and Kahma 2008) or different kinds of excluded groups, such as people with immigrant backgrounds or those who live in extreme poverty.

UNDERSTANDING CULTURAL NON-PARTICIPATION

This book has shown that certain classical debates regarding cultural stratification are still highly relevant, also in an egalitarian contexts such as Finland, and has argued that it is indeed still possible to claim that culture 'exists' or at least seems to be enjoyable for the people who have the resources to understand and properly decipher it. Cultural participation is not a question of accessibility or even personal motivation; rather, it is a matter of long-term embodied and resource-demanding exposure to highbrow-oriented culture. In the words of Bourdieu and Darbel (1991, 39): 'Access to works of art cannot be defined solely in terms of physical accessibility, since works of art exist only for those who have the means of understanding them'. Here, Bourdieu's point is that different cultural products do not even *exist* as cultural products or symbolic objects for groups that are unable to perceive them as such.

Education has traditionally been a key institution for cultivating this kind of ability to understand legitimate culture. Bourdieu's idea of cultural reproduction is that children assimilate cultural practices in their childhood homes and that later, the school system either punishes or rewards them for their 'natural' skills or the lack thereof, thus eventually transforming social hierarchies into academic and merit hierarchies (Bourdieu 1984/1979; Bourdieu 1993; Bourdieu and Passeron 1979). Mirroring this initial inequality, high education predicts active cultural participation across most national contexts (Bennett et al. 2009; García-Álvarez et al. 2007; Katz-Gerro and Jaeger 2013; López-Sintas and García-Álvarez 2002; Purhonen et al. 2014; Weingartner and Rössel 2019). Moreover, it seems that education has become an increasingly more significant predictor of both highbrow-oriented, mainstream and mundane cultural participation, also in Finland (Heikkilä and Lindblom 2022). Going back to my empirical results regarding the highly differentiated and partly hostile discourses on cultural participation, it could be interpreted that if differences are so noticeable in a traditionally highly egalitarian country with free public education such as Finland, they will larger still almost everywhere else, perhaps with the exception of the other Nordic countries.

In this scenario, and considering the fact that practically all people participate in everyday or popular culture in some ways, are there any viable ways of making people participate more in (highbrow-oriented) culture? Bourdieu and Darbel (1991) proposed levelling access to high culture institutions, such as museums, by offering visitors different verbal or textual 'codes', or explanations, that would help them navigate previously unfamiliar cultural experiences, thus creating 'an implicit recognition of the right not to understand and to demand to understand' (Bourdieu and Darbel 1991, 94). Bourdieu and Darbel also suggested things that today are commonplace in nearly all museums: catalogues, ground plans, shops, bars, restaurants and so on. However, it is unclear whether, and most probably unlikely that, these attempts to make highbrow-oriented cultural participation more accessible or democratic really manage to make audiences less culturally differentiated than before (Bennett 1995). This also means that many well-intentioned endeavours meant to lower access barriers to high culture may be useless or may only engage people who are already likely participants (see Jancovich and Ejgod Hansen 2018). Bourdieu and Darbel (1991, 102) went on to argue that 'there is no short cut to the path leading to the works of culture, and artificially produced (…) encounters (…) with them have no future'. Thus, encouraging people to participate in highbrow-oriented culture will likely not work through quick fixes such as lowering ticket prices, bringing culture physically closer to the people or so forth.

We perhaps too often pose the question about cultural participation incorrectly, by asking why certain people or groups do *not* participate in (highbrow-oriented) culture. We might as well ask: Why should they? Does (again, highbrow-oriented) cultural participation offer the people participating the least a mirror for their own experiences—that is, are people like themselves represented either in cultural production or in the cultural items themselves? Does cultural participation mean being at ease and enjoying themselves without feelings of alienation for the people who participate the least? Does public education offer, at least in theory, equal resources for everyone to understand and discern different forms of cultural participation—in other words, do people have more or less similar chances of extracting cultural capital from participating in culture and using it elsewhere in society for their benefit? If the answer to all or some of these questions is negative, it is no wonder that certain groups refrain from highbrow-oriented cultural participation.

I am tempted to ask, although in a provocative way, whether it is possible or even worthwhile to try to impose highbrow-oriented cultural participation on all citizens. What is the problem if some people have either literally or metaphorically 'gone fishing' instead of going to the opera or to the theatre? For a person from an underprivileged class position, choosing not to participate in highbrow-oriented culture is, perhaps, only a logical reaction in a society that puts high value on education and individual success. The people who refrain from participating in highbrow-oriented culture seem to know or to estimate that such participation will not give them either pleasurable experiences or useful capitals; rather, it will simply make them feel out of place, bored or angry. Engaging the least participating audiences cannot be approached as a matter of cultural policy alone—it is related to much broader structures of equality and belonging. The best possibilities for equalising or at least balancing cultural participation lie in an equal society, particularly when it comes to education, in avoiding marginalisation and in offering 'ownership' of culture to different kinds of underprivileged groups which are not an excluded minority but rather a silent majority. Understanding this is key in our societies characterised by cultural divides. In fact, if there are such steep differences regarding cultural participation and non-participation in the discourses of underprivileged classes in an egalitarian society such as Finland, these differences will only be larger elsewhere.

REFERENCES

Back L (2015) Why Everyday Life Matters: Class, Community and Making Life Livable. *Sociology* 49(5): 820–836.

Belfiore E (2002) Art as a means of alleviating social exclusion: Does it really work? A critique of instrumental cultural policies and social impact studies in the UK. *International Journal of Cultural Policy* 8(1): 91–106.

Belfiore E and Bennett O (2008) *The social impact of the arts: an intellectual history*. Basingstoke: Palgrave.

Belfiore E and Bennett O (2010) Beyond the "Toolkit Approach": Arts Impact Evaluation Research and the Realities of Cultural Policy-Making. *Journal for Cultural Research* 14(2): 121–142.

Bennett T (1995) *The Birth of the Museum. History, Theory, Politics*. London: Routledge.

Bennett T, Savage M, Silva E, Warde A, Gayo-Cal M and Wright D (2009) *Culture, Class, Distinction*. London: Routledge.

Bjørnsen E (2012) Norwegian cultural policy – A civilising mission? The Cultural Rucksack and abstract faith in the transforming powers of the arts. *Poetics* 40(4): 382–404.

Bourdieu P (1984/1979) *Distinction. A Social Critique of the Judgment of Taste.* London: Routledge & Kegan Paul.

Bourdieu P (1993) *The Field of Cultural Production. Essays on Art and Literature.* New York: Columbia Press.

Bourdieu P (1998) *Masculine Domination.* Standford, CA: Stanford University Press.

Bourdieu P and Darbel A (1991) *The Love of Art: European Art Museums and Their Public.* Cambridge: Polity.

Bourdieu P and Passeron JC (1979) *The Inheritors: French Students and Their Relation to Culture.* Chicago, IL: University of Chicago Press.

Bunting C, Gilmore A and Miles A (2019) Calling participation to account: Taking part in the politics of method. In Belfiore E and Gibson L (eds) *Histories of Cultural Participation, Values and Governance.* London: Palgrave, pp. 183–210.

De Keere K (2020) Finding the moral space: Rethinking morality, social class and worldviews. *Poetics* 79: 101415.

Dubois V (2015) Cultural policy regimes in Western Europe. In Wright JD (ed) *International Encyclopedia of the Social & Behavioral Sciences, 2nd edition.* London: Elsevier, pp: 460–465.

Ebrey J (2016) The mundane and insignificant, the ordinary and the extraordinary: Understanding Everyday Participation and theories of everyday life. *Cultural Trends* 25(3): 158–168.

Feder T and Katz-Gerro T (2015) The cultural hierarchy in funding: Government funding of the performing arts based on ethnic and geographic distinctions. *Poetics* 49: 76–95.

Flemmen, M, Jarness, V and Rosenlund, L (2018) Social space and cultural class divisions: The forms of capital and contemporary lifestyle differentiation. *British Journal of Sociology* 69(1): 124–153.

García-Álvarez E, Katz-Gerro T and López-Sintas J (2007) Deconstructing cultural omnivorousness 1982–2002: Heterology in Americans' musical preferences. *Social Forces* 86(2): 417–443.

Gest J (2016). *The new minority. White working class politics in an age of immigration and inequality.* Oxford: Oxford University Press.

Gilmore A (2017). The park and the commons: vernacular spaces for everyday participation and cultural value. *Cultural Trends* 26(1): 34-46.

Harrits GS and Pedersen HH (2019) Symbolic Class Struggles and the Intersection of Socioeconomic, Cultural and Moral Categorisations. *Sociology* 53(5): 861–878.

Heikkilä R (2021) The slippery slope of cultural non-participation: Orientations of participation among the potentially passive. *European Journal of Cultural Studies* 24: 202–219.

Heikkilä R and Kahma N (2008) Defining legitimate taste in Finland: Does mother tongue matter? *Research on Finnish Society* 1: 29–42.

Heikkilä R and Katainen A (2021) Counter-talk as symbolic boundary drawing: Challenging legitimate cultural practices in individual and focus group interviews in the lower regions of social space. *Sociological Review* 69: 1029–1050.

Heikkilä R and Lindblom T (2022) Overlaps and accumulations: The anatomy of cultural non-participation in Finland, 2007 to 2018. *Journal of Consumer Culture*. Available at: https://doi.org/10.1177/14695405211062052 (Accessed 21 August 2022).

Hennion A (2007) Those Things That Hold Us Together: Taste and Sociology. *Cultural Sociology* 1(1): 97–114.

Hochschild AR (2016) *Strangers in Their Own Land*. New York: The New Press.

Häyrynen S (2006) *Suomalaisen yhteiskunnan kulttuuripolitiikka.* [*Cultural policy of the Finnish society.*] SoPhi, (99). Jyväskylä: Minerva Kustannus.

Jancovich L (2017) The participation myth. *International Journal of Cultural Policy* 23(1): 107–121.

Jancovich L and Ejgod Hansen L (2018) Rethinking participation in the Aarhus as European Capital of Culture 2017 project. *Cultural Trends* 27(3): 173–186.

Jarness V (2015) Modes of consumption: From 'what' to 'how' in cultural stratification research. *Poetics* 53: 65–79.

Jarness V and Flemmen M (2019) A struggle on two fronts: Boundary drawing in the lower region of the social space and the symbolic market for "down-to-earthness". *British Journal of Sociology* 70: 166–189.

Jerolmack C and Khan S (2014) Talk is cheap: Ethnography and the attitudinal fallacy. *Sociological Methods and Research* 43(2): 178–209.

Kantola A, Aaltonen S, Haikkola L, Junnilainen L, Luhtakallio E, Patana P, Timonen J and Tuominen P (2022) *Kahdeksan kuplan Suomi. Yhteiskunnan muutosten syvät tarinat [Finland's eight bubbles. The deep stories of societal changes].* Gaudeamus: Helsinki.

Katz-Gerro T and Jaeger MM (2013) Top of the pops, ascend of the omnivores, defeat of the couch potatoes: Cultural consumption profiles in Denmark 1975–2004. *European Sociological Review* 29(2): 243–260.

Kvale S and Brinkmann S (2009) *InterViews. Learning the craft of qualitative research interviews.* London: Sage.

Lamont M (2000) *Dignity of Working Men. Morality and the Boundaries of Race, Class, and Immigration.* Cambridge: Harvard University Press.

Lamont M and Swidler A (2014) Methodological pluralism and the possibilities and limits of interviewing. *Qualitative Sociology* 37(2): 153–171.

López-Sintas J and García-Alvarez E (2002) Omnivores show up again: The segmentation of cultural consumers in the Spanish social space. *European Sociological Review* 183(3): 353–368.

McKenzie L (2015) *Getting By. Estates, Class and Culture in Austerity Britain.* London: Policy Press.

Mangset P (2020) The end of cultural policy? *International Journal of Cultural Policy* 26(3): 398– 411.

Miles A and Gibson L (2016) Everyday participation and cultural value. *Cultural Trends* 25(3): 151–157.

Miles A and Sullivan A (2012) Understanding participation in culture and sport: Mixing methods, reordering knowledges. *Cultural Trends* 21(4): 311–324.

Milling J (2019) Valuing cultural participation: The usefulness of the eighteenth-century stage. In: Belfiore E and Gibson L (eds) *Histories of Cultural Participation, Values and Governance.* London: Palgrave Macmillan, pp. 17–41.

Ollivier M (2008) Modes of openness to cultural diversity. Humanist, populist, practical, and indifferent. *Poetics* 36 (2–3): 120–147.

Prieur A and Savage M (2013) Emerging forms of cultural capital. *European Societies* 15(2): 246–267.

Purhonen S, Gronow J, Heikkilä R, Kahma N, Rahkonen K, Toikka A (2014) *Suomalainen maku: Kulttuuripääoma, kulutus ja elämäntyylien sosiaalinen eriytyminen [Finnish taste: Cultural capital, consumption and the social differentiation of lifestyles].* Helsinki: Gaudeamus.

Savage M, Cunningham N, Devine F, Friedman S, Laurison D, McKenzie L, Miles A, Snee H and Wakeling P (2015) *Social Class in the 21st Century.* London: Pelican.

Scott J C (1985) *Weapons of the Weak: Everyday Forms of Peasant Resistance.* New Haven: Yale University Press.

Skeggs B and Loveday V (2012) Struggles for Value: Value Practices, Injustice, Judgment, Affect and the Idea of Class. *The British Journal of Sociology* 63(3): 472–490.

Stevenson D (2013) What's the problem again? The problematisation of cultural participation in Scottish cultural policy. *Cultural Trends* 22(2): 77–85.

Stevenson D (2019) The cultural non-participant: Critical logics and discursive subject identities. *Arts and the Market* 9(1): 50–64.

Taylor M (2016) Nonparticipation or Different styles of Participation? Alternative Interpretations from Taking Part. *Cultural Trends* 25(3): 169–181.

Van Oorschot W (2006) Making the difference in social Europe: deservingness perceptions among citizens of European welfare states. *Journal of European Social Policy* 16(1): 23–42.

Van Oorschot W (2000) Who Should Get What, and Why? On Deservingness Criteria and the Conditionality of Solidarity among the Public. *Policy and Politics* 28 (1): 33–49.

Vassenden A and Jonvik M (2019) Cultural Capital as a Hidden Asset: Culture, Egalitarianism and Inter-Class Social Encounters in Stavanger, Norway. *Cultural Sociology* 13(1): 37–56.

Weingartner S and Rössel J (2019) Changing dimensions of cultural consumption? The space of lifestyles in Switzerland from 1976 to 2013. *Poetics* 74: 101345.

Willekens M and Lievens J (2016) Who participates and how much? Explaining non-attendance and the frequency of attending arts and heritage activities. *Poetics* 56: 50–63.

Correction to: Understanding Cultural Non-Participation in an Egalitarian Context

CORRECTION TO:

R. Heikkilä, *Understanding Cultural Non-Participation in an Egalitarian Context*, Palgrave Studies in Cultural Participation, https://doi.org/10.1007/978-3-031-18865-7

All chapters were previously published non-open access. They have now been changed to open access under a CC BY 4.0 license and the copyright holders for each chapter updated to 'The Author(s)'. The book has also been updated with these changes.

The updated original version for this book can be found at
https://doi.org/10.1007/978-3-031-18865-7

C2

Appendices

Sampling and Data Collection Procedure

The data collection was based on a theoretical sample of interviewees with background factors that statistically predicted low cultural participation. Two nationally representative surveys, *Culture and Leisure in Finland 2007* (N = 1388) and *Finnish Views on and Engagement in Culture and the Arts 2013* (N = 7859), were chosen for this purpose. Both are freely available through the Finnish Social Science Data Archive. The following two survey questions were used to measure non-participation: these were (1) *We will next enumerate different places and events. How often do you visit them?* and (2) *Which places related to culture and the arts have you visited in the following time span?* The cultural items listed included both 'highbrow' and 'lowbrow' items, ranging from opera and ballet to classical music, movies, rock concerts, pop events, folk dance events, restaurants, pubs and bingo. The alternatives indicating the frequency of participation ranged from 'every week' (*Culture and Leisure in Finland 2007*) or 'during the last six months' (*Finnish Views on and Engagement in Culture and the Arts 2013*) to 'rarely' and 'never' (formulations used by both surveys). A scale was constructed of the groups that never or very rarely participated in all the listed activities and compared against the background variables of the full data sets to formulate a sample that would mirror the factors most efficiently predicting cultural non-participation.

© The Author(s) 2022, corrected publication 2023   155
R. Heikkilä, *Understanding Cultural Non-Participation in an Egalitarian Context*, Palgrave Studies in Cultural Participation,
https://doi.org/10.1007/978-3-031-18865-7

Statistically significant factors for 'never' or 'very rarely' attending cultural activities were especially *education* (with low education predicting low participation), *residential area* (with living far from large cities predicting low participation), *occupation* (with manual workers being the likeliest non-participants) and *province* (with living in northern and eastern Finland predicting low participation). Other statistically significant predictors of low cultural participation included *being on pension, being a farmer, being unemployed* and *being on parental leave*. Age and gender were less significant factors.

The sample was formed with the idea that each interviewee would cover at least four statistically significant indicators of low cultural participation. Education was given priority as the most important variable conditioning cultural participation, which meant that no interviewed person had a full university degree. Some compromises were made regarding residential area and province: thus, approximately one third of the interviewees were recruited from the Helsinki metropolitan area. Altogether 42 individual interviews and 10 focus group interviews were originally collected, but three interviews were excluded from the data set because the informants had full university degrees. The data used in this book is comprised of 40 individual interviews and 9 focus groups, which were all collected in spring 2018.

The sample was carefully anonymised, and all identifiable information, such as names of people, cities and exact locations, was removed and modified to guarantee full anonymity. Whenever the interviews have included identifiable details such as extremely rare professions or hobbies, they were blurred or slightly modified. In this book, the interviewees were assigned the same pseudonyms as in my other publications based on the same data.

THE INTERVIEWEES

To facilitate the reading of the book, the interviewees are listed below in alphabetical order according to their pseudonyms. All interviewees were asked to fill in a background information sheet with information regarding their age, education, homes, possible occupation and their parents' occupations. Their places of residence were categorised as large metropoles (over 500,000 inhabitants), big cities (100,000 to 500,000 inhabitants), medium-sized cities (10,000 to 100,000 inhabitants), small cities (500 to 10,000 inhabitants) and countryside (fewer than 500 inhabitants). The interviewees' genders should be clear from the pseudonyms and pronouns used. It should be noted that some interviewees left one or several blank spaces into the background information sheets.

The Individual Interviewees

Aleksi, 29, has attended polytechnic university. He works as a sports instructor but is currently on parental leave. His father is a surveyor and his mother a bookkeeper. He lives in a medium-sized city.

Alma, 69, has attended basic school. She has worked as a farmer's wife but is now on pension. Her father was a train man and her mother a cemetery worker. She lives in the countryside.

Anniina, 39, has attended vocational school. She has worked as a salesperson but is now unemployed. Her father is a welder and her mother an office worker. She lives in a large metropole.

Eero, 30, has attended vocational school. He currently works as a kiosk salesperson. His father is a janitor and his mother a laboratory aide. He lives in a big city.

Eeva, 65, has attended vocational school. She has worked as a nurse but is now on pension. Her both parents were farmers. She lives in a big city.

Emilia, 21, has attended vocational school. She has worked as an electrician but is currently unemployed. Her father is a machinery man and her mother an office worker. She lives in a small city.

Emma, 34, has attended polytechnic university to become an engineer but is currently unemployed. Her father works as a salesperson and her mother as a services manager. She lives in a big city.

Ester, 39, has a bachelor's degree. She currently works as a salesperson. Her both parents are farmers. She lives in a small city.

Heidi, 26, has attended vocational school. She currently works as a practical nurse. Her father is a bus driver and her mother a practical nurse. She lives in a medium-sized city.

Hely, 59, has attended vocational school. She has worked in mixed manual jobs (for instance, as a salesperson and cook) but is now on disability pension. Her both parents were farmers. She lives in the countryside.

Henrik, 68, has attended vocational school. He worked as a traffic contractor but is now on pension. His both parents were farmers. He lives in a big city.

Iina, 45, has attended vocational school. She currently works as a shopkeeper. Her both parents are farmers. She lives in a small city.

Jarmo, 67, has attended vocational school. He has worked in mixed manual jobs (for instance, as a car painter, a car mechanic and a metal worker) but is now on pension. His father was a work supervisor and his mother a housewife. He lives in a big city.

Joni, 35, has a bachelor's degree. He has never worked anywhere and is on disability pension. His father is a teacher and his mother a social worker. He lives in a big city.

Julia, 68, has attended vocational school. She has worked as a hairdresser but is now on pension. Her father was a carpenter and her mother a housewife. She lives in a big city.

Lasse, 56, has attended vocational school. He has worked in mixed manual jobs (for instance, as a warehouse worker and as a construction worker) but is now unemployed. His father was a building engineer and his mother a kitchen helper. He lives in a large metropole.

Laura, 28, has attended vocational school. She currently works as a bus driver. Her mother is a worker in a photo lab. She lives in a large metropole.

Linda, 30, has attended sixth form. She is a student at the university but is currently on parental leave. Her father works at the post office and her mother a librarian. She lives in a big city.

Lukas, 41, has attended a commercial institute. He has worked as an office manager but is now unemployed. His both parents are unemployed. He lives in a large metropole.

Kaisa, 54, has attended domestic science school. She is currently working as a ward domestic. Her both parents were farmers. She lives in the countryside.

Karla, 40, has attended a polytechnic university. She has worked as a masseuse but is currently on parental leave. Her father is a farmer and her mother a housewife. She lives in the countryside.

Kimmo, 43, has attended vocational school. Currently he is on disability pension. His father is a renovator and his mother an office worker. He lives in a large metropole.

Maarit, 37, has attended vocational school to become a practical nurse but currently studies in a polytechnic university to become a physiotherapist. Her father works in the IT business and her mother an engineer. She lives in a large metropole.

Marketta, 69, has attended vocational school. She has worked as a guard but is now on pension. Her both parents were farmers. She lives in a large metropole.

Max, 39, has attended vocational school. He has worked in several mixed low-skilled jobs (for instance, as a car seller) but is now unemployed. His father is a storeman and his mother a cook. He lives in a large metropole.

Maria, 47, has attended vocational school. She currently works as a nurse. Her father was a carpenter and her mother a housewife. She lives in a medium-sized city.

Marko, 47, has attended basic school. He works as a farmer, and both his parents were farmers. He lives in the countryside.

Melissa, 27, has attended basic school. She has never worked anywhere and is on disability pension. She lives in a big city.

Mimosa, 37, has attended vocational school. She currently works as a cleaner. Her father is a renovator and her mother a cleaner. She lives in a large metropole.

Minna, 38, has attended vocational school. She is currently a manual worker on parental leave. Her father is a head butcher and her mother a practical nurse. She lives in a large metropole.

Oliver, 34, has attended vocational school. He has worked in various jobs (for instance, in an office and selling Christmas trees) but is now unemployed. His father is an IT developer and his mother a nurse. He lives in a large metropole.

Olli, 41, has attended vocational school. He currently works as a machine operator. His father is an entrepreneur and his mother a secretary. He lives in a large metropole.

Petteri, 34, has attended sixth form. He currently works as a truck driver. His father is a truck driver and his mother a cleaner. He lives in a small city.

Sami, 37, has attended vocational school. He currently works as a cook. His both parents are food workers. He lives in a medium-sized city.

Sara, 33, has attended basic school. She has worked as a salesperson but is now unemployed. Her father is unemployed and her mother a director of an association. She lives in a large metropole.

Sebastian, 28, has attended basic school. He has never worked anywhere and is unemployed. His mother works in customer service. He lives in a medium-sized city.

Silja, 64, has attended vocational school. She has worked in mixed manual jobs (for instance, as a messenger, as a house janitor and as a cleaner) and is now on pension. Her father was a logger and her mother a housewife. She lives in a large metropole.

Tarja, 59, has attended sixth form. She has worked as a secretary but is now unemployed. Her father was a road work boss and her mother a home aid. She lives in a large metropole.

Tuomo, 77, has attended vocational school. He has worked as an engineer but is now on pension. His both parents were farmers. He lives in a big city.

Ville, 35, has attended vocational school. He has worked as a welder but is now unemployed. His father is a truck driver and his mother a cleaner. He lives in a large metropole.

The Focus Groups
FG1: Female students at a vocational school in a big city

Katja, 18, has attended basic school and is now studying to become a practical nurse. Her father is a practical nurse and her mother a childminder.

Sonja, 18, has attended basic school and is now studying to become a practical nurse. Her father is a driving instructor and her mother a practical nurse.

FG2: Male students at a vocational school in a big city

Eetu, 17, has attended basic school and is now studying to become an electrician. His father is an electrician and his mother a cook.

Onni, 18, has attended basic school and is now studying to become an electrician. His father is an entrepreneur and his mother a nurse.

Otso, 17, has attended basic school and is now studying to become an electrician. His father is an electrician and his mother a nurse.

Tom, 17, has attended basic school and is now studying to become an electrician. His father is an machinery man and his mother a secretary.

Vilho, 17, has attended basic school and is now studying to become an electrician. His father is a plumber and his mother a practical nurse.

FG3: Pensioner couple and their daughter in a big city

Elina, 33, has attended a polytechnic university. She is a childminder currently on parental leave. Her father was a sales manager and her mother a nurse.

Esko, 64, has attended vocational school. He worked as a sales manager but is now on pension. His father was a porter and his mother a cleaner.

Malla, 64, has attended vocational school. She worked as a nurse but is now on pension. Her father was and engineer and her mother a housewife.

FG4: Working-class couple in a medium-sized city

Jarkko, 27, has attended a polytechnic university. He currently works as an engineer. His father is a carpenter and his mother a teacher.

Milla, 27, is a student at a vocational school. Her father is a truck driver and her mother a practical nurse.

FG5: Association of unemployed people in a medium-sized city

Eemeli, 61, has attended vocational school. He has worked as a car driver but is now unemployed. His father was a car driver and his mother a housewife.

Eki, 53, has attended vocational school. He has worked as a carpenter but is now unemployed. His father was a carpenter and his mother a housewife.

Kalle, 58, has been a sawmill worker but is now unemployed. His father was a construction blaster.

Miko, 32, has attended vocational school. He has worked as a salesperson but is now unemployed. His both parents are on pension.

Oskari, 60, is unemployed. His father worked as a pastry-cook and his mother as a cleaner.

Santeri, 58, is a Bachelor of Arts. He has worked as a teacher but is now unemployed. His both parents were teachers.

Ukko, 33, has attended vocational school. He has worked as a mechanic but is now unemployed. His both parents are farmers.

FG6: Municipal rehabilitative work group in a medium-sized city

Anneli, 49, has attended vocational school. She has worked as a practical nurse but is now unemployed. Her father was a teacher and her mother a secretary.

Lauri, 58, has attended polytechnic university. He has worked as an engineer but is now unemployed. His father was a technician and his mother a specialist in the healthcare sector.

Matti, 59, has attended polytechnic university. He has worked as a researcher but is now unemployed. His father was a foreman and his mother a housewife.

Rob, 57, is unemployed. He does not provide any information about his education or possible previous occupation or his parents' occupations.

Teppo, 53, has attended vocational school. He has been a construction worker but is now unemployed. His father was a carpenter and his mother a cleaner.

FG7: Regulars of a local bar of a small city

Johanna, 55, has attended vocational school and is a manual worker. Her father has been a conductor and her mother a childminder.

Raisa, 40, has attended vocational school and works as a cook. Her father is a cook and her mother a school cook.

Simo, 53, has worked as an hourly teacher but is now on pension. His father was a mason and his mother a teacher.

FG8: Pensioners' association in a small city

Anja, 64, has attended vocational school and been a park worker. Her father was a logger and her mother a housewife.

Ensio, 65, has attended sixth form and worked as a technician. His father was a clerk and his mother a cleaner.

Johan, 78, has attended vocational school and worked as a clerk. His mother was a housewife.

Pekka, 72, has attended basic school and worked in a paper mill. His father was an employee representative of the paper mill and his mother a foodstuff worker.

Sally, 80, has attended vocational school and worked as a bus driver.

Veijo, 82, has been a social worker. His father was a shopkeeper and his mother a housewife.

FG9: Farmer and his family/friends

Timo, 51, has attended high school and is a farmer. Both his parents were farmers.

Salla, 43, has attended polytechnic university. She is a farmer's wife. Her father was an excavator driver and her mother a seamstress.

Elsa, 84, has attended college and worked as a teacher. Her father was a railway station master and her mother a housewife.

INTERVIEW GUIDELINES

The interviews were unstructured and open-ended, and they were organised around broad topics discussed in the following order:

1. Home, family, friends
2. School, studies
3. Working life
4. Leisure, hobbies, holidays, free time
5. Cultural areas: food, music, reading, TV, cinema

6. Photo elicitation: looking at eleven pictures of Finnish classical artworks[1] and discussing them
7. Participation in different events (closed-ended list of participation in events such as fairs, exhibitions, flea markets, bingo, sports events, cinema, concerts and so forth)
8. "Day of my dreams" (open-ended discussion of what the participant would most like to do during one day if there were no limitations

[1] Schjerfbeck: *Toipilas*
[2] Rafael Wardi: *Asetelma*
[3] Ekman: *Ilmatar*
[4] Gallen-Kallela: *Poika ja varis*
[5] Bäck: *Sodan sävel*
[6] Halonen: *Talvimaisema*
[7] Thesleff: *Omakuva*
[8] Osipow: *Punainen parooni*
[9] Kaivanto: *Kun meri kuolee*
[10] Saanio: *Suru ilman mustia vaatteita*
[11] Von Wright: *Taistelevat metsot*

The manufacturer's authorised representative in the EU is Springer
Nature Customer Service Centre GmbH, Europaplatz 3, 69115 Heidelberg,
Germany. If you have any concerns regarding our products, please
contact ProductSafety@springernature.com

Printed and bound by CPI Group (UK) Ltd, Croydon, CR0 4YY
29/04/2026
02099525-0009